Divine Desserts

Divine Desserts

BERNICE HURST

GUILD PUBLISHING
LONDON

Opposite: Sundae supreme

A QUINTET BOOK

This edition published 1986 by
Book Club Associates
by arrangement with
Quintet Publishing Ltd

This book was designed and produced by
Quintet Publishing Limited
6 Blundell Street, London N7

Art director Peter Bridgewater
Editor Polly Powell
Photographer Trevor Wood and Mike Bull
Home Economists Felicity Jeliff and Brenda
Smith

Typeset in Great Britain by
Central Southern Typesetters, Eastbourne
Colour origination in Hong Kong by
Universal Colour Scanning Limited
Printed in Hong Kong by
Leefung-Asco Printers Limited

The publishers would like to thank Christmas
Archives and Photo Library for the illustrations
on pages 6-9, 11 (above) and 13.

Contents

INTRODUCTION   6

CHEESECAKES   14

CREPES   26

PASTRY   36

FRUIT   54

CHOCOLATE   72

ICE CREAM   88

SOUFFLES   106

PUDDINGS   116

INDEX   128

H ISTORICALLY, the temptation of a sweet goes back to Eve and that well-known apple. Cooks rarely had the wide choice of ingredients we have today and had to be satisfied with using only a very few basic ingredients. Desserts were made from what was readily to hand, but think of what was done with them!

It is understandable that even so-called traditional desserts today vary from one kitchen to another. Back in the old days there were no recipe books; the only way to learn was to cook. Not everyone was willing to share a recipe. Desserts were created and recreated, tasted, copied and altered. Even when recipes were passed on, instructions were often verbal and subject to both deliberate and accidental alteration. Each cook had to produce a flavour and texture that was acceptable, not to say enjoyable, through simple trial and error.

Today we do not have these problems. There is an abundance of cookbooks, some with original recipes, others perpetuating old favourites. Fresh ingredients are available – although frequently at a price – all the year round. We are not restricted to ingredients native to our location. Freezing and canning preserve the quality of those things which we cannot obtain fresh. Flavourings and spices can be used at will. We can experiment and create our own desserts, but it is interesting to see what other people have done in the past and are doing now to finish their meals . . .

Let's look at some of those basic ingredients and see how they have been used. Desserts are by their very nature sweet, but sugar was not commonly used until the 17th and 18th centuries. Prior to that, it was to be found in only the richest of homes. There is good reason for the association of desserts with ambrosia, and for sweet drinks to be called "the nectar of the gods". None but the most well-to-do could afford to have their cooks present sweet dishes. Sugar loaf was at one time considered a sign of wealth. Desserts were status symbols and in Victorian England and Europe they were set out with great fanfare. At the end of a lavish meal an entire buffet was wheeled in by white-gloved major domos. Ice-cream sculptures, glittering jellies, pastry masterpieces, charlottes and meringues were all created as much to impress as to enjoy.

Antonin Carême, that most respected chef, produced not only elaborate compositions such as the unforgettable Charlotte Russe and Bavarian creams but also his renowned pastry sculptures used as set pieces at banquets. They were the ultimate in centrepieces; there to

Right: The original Pennsylvania Dutch assorted cookies
Opposite: The traditional iced birthday cake

Divine Desserts
INTRODUCTION

8

be admired and to serve a decorative function only. Not long ago, the grand finale of a wedding or a banquet in American catering halls was called a Viennese table. After the main course had been cleared away the lights were dimmed and a team of waiters rolled in trolley after trolley ladened with more desserts than even the greediest guests could sample, try though they might. The affluence of the host was proved.

What, then, did the rest of us eat for dessert? Honey has been around for a long time and so, of course, has fruit with all its natural sugar goodness. In North America the Indians taught the European settlers how to tap the maple tree to extract its syrup. Sweet vegetables, such as yams and pumpkins, were frequently used as the basis of desserts in North and South America as well as in parts of Africa and the South Pacific. When one craves sugar, there are ways and means of finding it the world over!

Among the earliest recorded desserts were drinks made of wine, fruit juice or honey and served over crushed ice. Here lie the origins of the *sharbats* of Persia, the *frio frio* popular in the Caribbean, the *granita* of Italy and the *granité* of France. The Romans were said to have tried snow with wine and fruit toppings. Crushed or cracked ice mixed with pieces of fruit or topped with a fruit syrup could, perhaps, be called the first natural or wholefood desserts – there was, of course, nothing added or taken away from the ingredients as Mother Nature had provided them. Early desserts in Britain were also liquid – possets, caudles and syllabub were variations created on the theme of wine, eggs and cream. Foamy sauces of similar ingredients led to *sabayon* in France, *zabaione* in Italy and *weinschaumsaucen* in Germany. In tropical countries the coconut and its milk were the base for sweet drinks and snacks. In China desserts were only served on special occasions. For every-day meals, there were simply sweet teas made, for example, from almonds and pineapple as part of the meal. At that time, when the ingredients available were limited, it was only natural that similar desserts should appear on tables in disparate places all over the world.

Fruit was a common factor in developing desserts. Although fresh fruit truly needs no glorification, the temptation to use it for experimentation was irresistible. Fruit sauces thickened with cornflour (cornstarch), sago, rice and semolina abounded. If there were no dairy products to be had, a pudding could still be concocted from fruit and grits or porridge. Later on, jelly was used to set the sauces and beautifully moulded (molded) puddings began to appear. The variations on *flummery, flammeri, rote grütze, rodgrod* etc. from Britain, Germany and Denmark, to name but a few, cannot be counted.

Above: A Venetian villa of pâte d'office (sweet paste) and nougat
Opposite: A 19th-century interpretation of a medieval banqueting scene

If there were egg-laying or milk-giving animals to hand, the possibilities were even more exciting. Fruit and cheese have always been an interesting mix. From the moulded (molded) *pashka* of Russia to the fruit tarts of French *pâtissières*, from Italian pastries filled with cheese and crystallized fruit to eastern European cheesecakes, fruit and dairy products have always been an appetizing combination. The simplest combinations of whipped cream cheese and chunks of fresh fruit or chopped, poached and puréed fruit mixed with fresh or sour cream can be delicious. Sorbets (sherbets) and ice creams, lightened with egg whites and enriched with cream, are a delight. Yoghurt (yogurt) has been used with fruit for desserts in Persia and its surrounds for hundreds of years. Today, along with *fromage frais* in France, *ricotta* in Italy and other low fat cheeses in England and America, it satisfies our, perhaps contradictory, desire for healthy desserts.

Methods of preserving fruit were developed very early on. Sun-dried figs, raisins, dates and apricots sweetened Middle Eastern desserts all the year round. Elsewhere, rum pots were popular. These were large crocks filled with layers of fruit left to soak in rum or brandy. The pots were topped up constantly but, perhaps, not as

Above: An early confectioner's workshop specialising in the production of plain (see figure 1) and beaded (see figure 2) sugarplums. Candies were originally sweetened with honey and only later with sugar. Nuts or small slices of fruit shaken in melted gum arabic would then be coated alternately with sugar and gum. Figure 3 shows almonds being shaken over a barrel and figure 4 is a bowl for finished beaded sugarplums.

quickly as their contents were devoured. Fruit, boiled down to make jams and preserves, was often served by the spoonful with a cup of tea or coffee. This custom persists in Jewish and Muslim homes throughout the Middle East and Eastern Europe as well as in the homes of *émigrés* from these countries.

Fruit salads could be the subject of an encyclopaedia. Combinations of fresh fruit, soaked in lemon juice or wine, served alone or with sauces are matched only by combinations of poached fruit for compotes or mixtures of fresh, dried and crystallized fruit. Fruit can be arranged in the most exquisite patterns as those exponents of nouvelle cuisine have shown us, and mint leaves, lemon balm, flowers and nuts can all be used as garnishes. Flavourings should complement and enhance the fruit rather than overwhelming it. The combinations of flavours are literally infinite.

Fruit is used in many more ways than those already outlined. The Austrians, for instance, have their dumplings – whole plums wrapped in a pastry made of cooked

potatoes and flour and then fried or poached. These bear no small resemblance to the British pudding – fruit mixed with a suet crust, wrapped in a cloth and boiled for many hours. In France, one of the simplest family desserts consists of sliced fruit sprinkled with sugar and set on a slice of *brioche*. The *croûton* is baked until the fruit is tender and the sugar bubbles. Fruit can be, has been, and probably will be used for fritters, crêpes, and pastries for evermore.

Cream has been used from earliest times for desserts. It can bind purées to make fools, lighten egg custards or be piped over any number of desserts to decorate and transform them. Flavoured creams can be used for the simplest and most elaborate of desserts. A few macaroon crumbs or chopped nuts can be whisked in, for example, but if you begin to experiment, there is no end to the creations you can place on the table. *Petits pots de crème*, mousses, trifles, and pastries all give the cook with time to spend an area for discovery and delight. *Konditorein* and *pâtisseries* are so enticing that they are popular not only for dessert, but with morning coffee and afternoon tea as well. We buy cream cakes for ourselves and as gifts for friends. When we have guests, we welcome them with something sweet. Cream desserts are a splendid way to end a meal, and oh, how rich and extravagant.

As for eggs, custards in their many shapes and textures are another basis for classic desserts the world

semolina. In Asia there is glutinous rice, often sweetened with bean paste. Rice and potato flours are used as well as wheat flour. In northern Europe grits, barley and oats provided early ingredients for puddings. Bread, too, is used in endless ways – sliced or crumbed, hollowed out and filled. Poor Knights are simply slices of bread dipped in egg and fried. Bread and butter puddings with the bread soaked in custard and chunks of spicy, fruity bread puddings are both English favourites.

These, then, are some of the basics, but what of those special, luxurious ingredients? What of chocolate, and even sugar itself? It is with these that pastry chefs and confectioners come into their own, creating edible baskets, sugar sculptures, and petits-fours. Not many of us have the time, patience or imagination to develop the skill needed to compete with the professionals in this field. These factors, perhaps, make us appreciate their desserts all the more – and try that much harder in our own kitchens! Desserts are usually an indulgence and as such should be planned carefully, prepared whole-heartedly, and enjoyed thoroughly.

Left: Willing hands in the kitchen
Below: The deplorable effect of pastries

over. They may be baked or of a pouring consistency, used to fill tarts or pastries and served hot or cold. Meringues can be poached or baked, filled or used as a base for the world-famous Pavlova. Italian meringue can be piped onto the outside of a Charlotte or Baked Alaska. The soufflé, that airy, crusty, delicate dessert, can be flavoured at will but must be treated with extreme care.

There are, of course, other ingredients that have always been to hand in one form or other – flour for batters to make crêpes and fritters, and for those fantastic pies that have been an American favourite since the time of the founding fathers. Puff and choux pastry are used in Europe for feather light confections containing custard, cream, butter cream, praline, jam or fruit. *strudel* pastry and *filo* of the Middle East are used to make layered desserts containing an array of fillings. Cereals, too, have been used for desserts – rice, sago and

Baking Trays

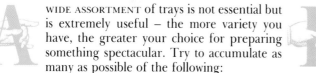

WIDE ASSORTMENT of trays is not essential but is extremely useful – the more variety you have, the greater your choice for preparing something spectacular. Try to accumulate as many as possible of the following:

☛ Swiss (jelly) roll pan or large flat baking sheet.

☛ Flan (pie) rings, preferably with loose bottoms. Metal pans conduct heat better than china pans, pretty though they may be.

☛ Deep and shallow pie plates and bun (muffin or cup cake) pans.

☛ Sandwich pans and cake pans in a variety of depths and sizes. Square and rectangular pans are useful as well as round pans. Where possible, use springform or loose-bottomed pans. Non-stick pans are good but have a limited life and need to be replaced regularly.
Although many of the baking pans listed above can be used as moulds, a few special ones are also useful. China, plastic or metal can be used but try to choose universal materials that are suitable for both baking and freezing.

☛ Moulds (molds) of varying sizes and *petit fours* moulds of different shapes and sizes are by no means necessary but can be incredibly useful for making a display of pastries.

☛ China soufflé dishes and ramekins (individual serving dishes) for soufflés, mousses and baked custards.

☛ A savarin or ring mould (mold), with straight or fluted edges, may not be used frequently, but there is no adequate substitute.

Mixing Utensils

LECTRIC MIXERS and food processors can save a great deal of time and effort. They are ideal for making pastry. Not all food processors are suitable for whisking eggs or cream so choose carefully.

☛ Whisks of different sizes and shapes are invaluable.

☛ A wire cake rack for cooling and an assortment of knives and palettes (metal spatulas) for smoothing edges, lifting biscuits off trays and spreading cream or icing.

☛ Pastry cutters of different sizes and shapes.

☛ *Cannelle* knife for cutting strips of orange or lemon peel.

☛ A small sharp knife for chopping fruit, cutting decorations, pastry, marzipan etc.

☛ Pastry brush, decorating comb, ice cream scoop, piping (pastry) bag and assorted nozzles are all used for glazing, decorating or making shapes of pastry, icing or cream.

☛ Bowls of assorted sizes.

☛ One or more measuring pots. Measuring cups and spoons are also a great help.

☛ A juice squeezer and a grater prove invaluable in the kitchen.

Opposite: The pastrycook's equipment in the 18th century. A selection of elaborate marzipan cutters, moulds (molds) for pastries and cookies, waffle irons and bread oven paddles.

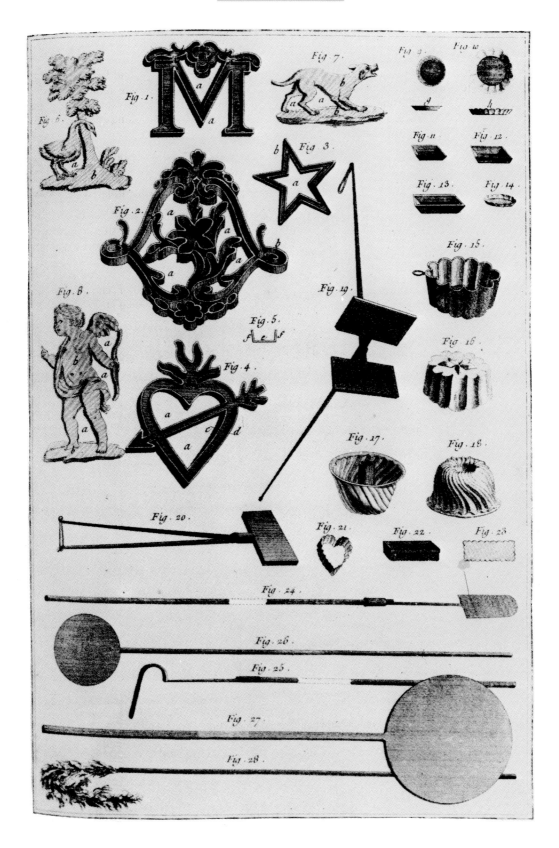

Cheesecakes

CHEESECAKE BASES   16

UNIVERSAL FILLINGS   16

MAIDS OF HONOUR   17

PINEAPPLE COCONUT CHEESECAKE   19

RAISIN CHEESECAKE   20

COTTAGE CHEESECAKE   21

ORANGE CHEESECAKE   22

ITALIAN CHEESECAKE   24

WEIGHT WATCHERS' CHEESECAKE   25

Opposite: Strawberry cheesecake

Introduction

ALTHOUGH CHEESECAKES have been around for centuries, they have recently undergone a remarkable upsurge in popularity. Several decades ago they were virtually unheard of in England, for example, despite the fact that Queen Elizabeth I enjoyed Maids of Honour regularly. With Americans leading the way, creative cooks all over the world have taken to experimenting with flavourings, fillings, bases and toppings to produce masterpieces worthy of the most discerning palates.

As with many desserts, cheesecakes originated in days when desserts had to be prepared from a limited range of ingredients. Cheese was, of course, widely available but, in Eastern Europe particularly, cheesecakes were often very tart, as fruit was the only ingredient readily to hand for sweetening. Textures varied widely – fresh butter could be used for pastry, fresh or sour cream was sometimes mixed with the cheese which itself could be creamy or in curd form. Buttermilk was frequently added for piquancy. Ground nuts and flower waters such as rose and orange were early additions in England.

Today we have no such limitations on ingredients and, therefore, no limitations on cheesecakes. We make cheesecakes because we love them and because there is no end to their variety. The following recipes may provide you with some new ideas – mix them up, as you like, to create your own favourites.

Cheesecake Bases

INGREDIENTS

CRUMB CRUST

2 cups/225 g/8 oz biscuit (cookie) crumbs

2 tbsp/25 g/1 oz sugar

½ tsp/2½ g cinnamon or nutmeg

4 tbsp/50 g/2 oz butter or margarine

PREPARATION

☛ Combine crumbs, sugar, spices and melted butter or margarine until the crumbs are moist but not sticky.
☛ Press over the base and partially up the sides of a 23 cm/9 in loose-bottomed pan.

INGREDIENTS

PASTRY CRUST

1 cup + 2 tbsp/100 g/4 oz plain (all-purpose) flour

a pinch of salt

4 tbsp/50 g/2 oz fat (shortening)

2 tbsp/30 ml cold water

PREPARATION

☛ Combine the flour and salt. Rub in the fat until the mixture resembles coarse breadcrumbs.
☛ Sprinkle over the water and bring the dough together with a knife. Add a few more drops of water if necessary but do not let the dough get too sticky.
☛ Chill, then roll out to line the base and sides of a 20 cm/8 in pan.
☛ For a sweeter pastry, stir 1 tbsp/15 g/½ oz sugar into the flour. A lightly beaten egg can be substituted for water.

Universal Fillings

INGREDIENTS

SERVES 6–8

1½ cups/350 g/12 oz cream cheese

2 eggs

½ cup/100 g/4 oz sugar

½ tsp/2½ ml vanilla essence (extract)

oven temperature 180°C/350°F/Gas 4

PREPARATION

☛ Beat the cheese until it is smooth. Add the remaining ingredients and mix well.
☛ Pour over the base of your choice and bake for 35 minutes.

VARIATION

4 cups/675 g/1½ lb curd (ricotta) cheese

1 lemon

2 eggs

6 tbsp/75 g/3 oz sugar

oven temperature 190°C/375°F/Gas 5

PREPARATION

☛ Beat the cheese until it is smooth. Add the juice of the lemon, eggs and sugar. Mix well.
☛ Pour over the base of your choice and bake for 20 minutes.

Maids of Honour

INGREDIENTS

SERVES 8

½ lb/225 g/8 oz puff pastry (see page 52)

apricot jam

1 cup/225 g/8 oz curd (ricotta) cheese

2 eggs

3 tbsp/40 g/1½ oz sugar

1 lemon

2 tbsp/25 g ground almonds

1 tbsp/15 g currants

oven temperature 200°C/400°F/Gas 6

PREPARATION

☛ Roll out the pastry and cut into eight rounds. Line tart tins (muffin or cupcake pans). Put a drop of jam into each.

☛ Beat the cheese until it is smooth. Add one whole egg plus the yolk of the second and mix well.

☛ Stir in the grated rind of the lemon and the ground almonds. Fold in the currants.

☛ Carefully spoon the filling into the prepared pastry cases (shells).

☛ Bake for 25 minutes. Serve cool but not chilled, topped with icing (confectioners') sugar.

Pineapple Coconut Cheesecake

INGREDIENTS

SERVES 8

BASE

4 tbsp/50 g/2 oz butter

1 tbsp/15 g sugar

1/2 cup/50 g/2 oz desiccated (shredded) coconut

1/3 cup/50 g/2 oz ground hazelnuts (filberts)

oven temperature 180°C/350°F/Gas 4

FILLING

450 g/1 lb curd (ricotta) cheese

2 tbsp/30 ml lemon juice

1 egg

2 tbsp/30 g sugar

oven temperature 190°C/375°F/Gas 5

TOPPING

1/2 cup/125 g/4 oz pineapple pieces

2 1/2 tsp/12 1/2 g cornflour (cornstarch)

1/2 cup/100 ml/4 fl oz pineapple juice

2 1/2 tsp/2 1/2 ml rum

1/2 cup/100 ml/4 fl oz water

1 tbsp/15 g desiccated (shredded) coconut

PREPARATION

☛ Melt the butter and stir into the other base ingredients. Press over the bottom and up the sides of a greased 20 cm/8 in pan.
☛ Bake for 5 minutes.
☛ Beat together all the filling ingredients. Pour onto the base.
☛ Bake for 20 minutes.
☛ Leave the cake to cool slightly before adding the topping. Arrange the pineapple pieces on top of the cake.
☛ Combine the cornflour, pineapple juice and rum. Heat, stirring constantly, until the glaze thickens and clears.
☛ Gently spoon the glaze over the fruit.

TO SERVE

Garnish the cheesecake by sprinkling with coconut.

Raisin Cheesecake

INGREDIENTS

SERVES 6—8

BASE

1 cup/125 g/4 oz digestive biscuits (Graham crackers)

3 tbsp/50 g/1½ oz butter

1 tbsp/15 g sugar

1 tsp/5 g cinnamon

FILLING

1 cup/225 g/8 oz cottage cheese

1 cup/225 g/8 oz curd (ricotta) cheese

2 eggs, separated

¼ cup/50 g/2 oz sugar

5 g/1 tsp lemon rind

⅓ cup/50 g/2 oz raisins

⅓ cup/50 g/2 oz sultanas (white raisins)

oven temperature 170°C/325°F/Gas 3

PREPARATION

☛ Crush the biscuits and mix with melted butter, sugar and cinnamon. Press over the base of a 20 cm/8 in pan.

☛ Strain the cottage cheese so that the lumps are as small as possible. Beat with the curd cheese until smooth.

☛ Mix the egg yolks with the cheese. Beat in the sugar and grated lemon rind and stir in the fruit.

☛ Beat the egg whites until they are stiff but not dry. Gently fold into the cheese mixture.

☛ Pour the filling onto the base and bake for 40 minutes. Cool in the oven with the door slightly open.

Cottage Cheesecake

INGREDIENTS

SERVES 6—8

BASE

½ cup/100 g/4 oz soft margarine

1½ cups/175 g/6 oz plain (all-purpose) flour

½ tsp/2½ g baking powder

¼ cup/50 g/2 oz sugar

1 lemon

FILLING

3 eggs, separated

½ cup/100 g/4 oz sugar

1½ cups/350 g/12 oz cottage cheese

⅔ cup/150 ml/5 fl oz soured (sour) cream

oven temperature 160°C/325°F/Gas 3

PREPARATION

☛ Beat together all the base ingredients to form a dough. Roll out gently to line the base and sides of a 20 cm/8 in pan.

☛ Beat the egg yolks with the sugar until they are nearly white.

☛ Strain the cheese and add to the egg yolks along with the soured cream. Mix well.

☛ Whisk the egg whites until they are stiff but not dry. Gently fold into the filling mixture starting with just one spoonful and gradually adding the remainder. Pour into the pastry case (shell).

☛ Bake for 50 minutes. Cool in the oven with the door slightly open. Chill before serving.

Orange Cheesecake

INGREDIENTS

SERVES 6—8
BASE
1 tbsp/15 g margarine
½ cup/50 g/2 oz dried breadcrumbs
FILLING
1 cup/225 g/8 oz cottage cheese
½ cup/100 g/4 oz cream cheese
2 eggs
⅓ cup/75 g/3 oz sugar
2 tbsp/30 g cornflour (cornstarch)
2 tsp/10 ml orange juice
½ tsp/2½ g orange rind
⅔ cup/150 ml/5 fl oz soured (sour) cream
4 tbsp/50 g/2 oz butter

oven temperature 170°C/325°F/Gas 3

PREPARATION

☛ Grease a 20 cm/8 in pan with the margarine. Sprinkle over the breadcrumbs and tilt the pan slightly so that the sides are coated.

☛ Chill while preparing the filling.

☛ Strain the cottage cheese and beat with the cream cheese until the mixture is fairly smooth. Add the eggs and sugar. Mix well.

☛ Stir in the cornflour, orange juice and grated orange rind. Gently stir in the soured cream and melted butter.

☛ Pour the filling onto the base and bake for 40 minutes or until firm to the touch.

☛ For a thicker cake, double all the ingredients and use a 23 cm/9 inch pan.

Italian Cheesecake

INGREDIENTS

SERVES 10–12

BASE

6 tbsp/75 g/3 oz butter

2 egg yolks

2 tbsp/25 g sugar

1 tbsp/15 ml Marsala

½ tsp/2½ g lemon rind

a pinch of salt

1 cup + 2 tbsp/100 g/4 oz plain (all-purpose) flour

FILLING

2 cups/450 g/1 lb curd (ricotta) cheese

¼ cup/50 g/2 oz sugar

1 tsp/5 g plain (all-purpose) flour

a pinch of salt

½ tsp/2½ ml vanilla essence (extract)

½ tsp/2½ g orange rind

2 egg yolks

1 tbsp/15 g sultanas (white raisins)

1 tbsp/15 g candied peel

1 tbsp/15 g chopped almonds

oven temperature 180°C/350°F/Gas 4

PREPARATION

☛ Mix all the base ingredients together until a dough has formed. Handle as little as possible while blending. Gently roll or press into shape and line the base and sides of a 23 cm/9 in loose-bottomed pan.

☛ Beat the cheese until it is smooth. Mix well with all the other ingredients, adding the fruit and nuts last of all. Pour into the pastry case.

☛ Bake for 45–50 minutes. Cool and dust with icing (confectioners') sugar before serving.

Weight Watchers' Cheesecake

INGREDIENTS

SERVES 6

BASE

6 tbsp/75 g/3 oz margarine

6 tbsp/75 g/3 oz sugar

¾ cup/75 g/3 oz plain (all-purpose) flour

2 tbsp/30 g cornflour (cornstarch)

oven temperature 160°C/325°F/Gas 3

FILLING

1 egg, separated

1 lemon

2 tbsp/30 ml milk

3 tbsp/45 g/1½ oz sugar

½ cup/125 g/4 oz skimmed milk cheese

½ cup/125 g/4 oz cottage cheese

⅔ cup/150 ml/¼ pt whipping cream

PREPARATION

☛ To make the shortbread base, rub the margarine into the combined sugar, flour and cornflour until it resembles coarse crumbs. Bind lightly and press over the base of a 20 cm/8 in pan.

☛ Prick and bake for 40 minutes. Combine the egg yolk, grated lemon rind, milk and sugar for the filling. Heat, stirring, until thick. Leave to cool.

☛ Beat the skimmed milk cheese until it is smooth. Strain the cottage cheese before adding to the skimmed milk cheese. Stir in the lemon juice.

☛ Whip the cream and gently fold into the cheese mixture.

☛ Whisk the egg white until it is stiff but not dry. Fold into the filling mixture, starting with just one spoonful and gradually adding the remainder.

☛ Pour the filling over the cool shortbread and chill until set.

TO SERVE

Serve with fresh fruit or a fruit topping.

Crêpes

BASIC CREPE BATTER 28

CREPE FILLINGS 29

CREPES SUZETTE 30

STRAWBERRY CHEESE CREPES 31

PANCAKE GATEAU 32

BLINTZES 33

AMERICAN BLUEBERRY PANCAKES 34

Opposite: Peach cheese crêpes
(see page 31)

Introduction

RÊPES ARE the perfect example of basic ingredients being used to create some of the most popular desserts. This simple mixture of flour, egg and milk can be served with unadorned accompaniments or transformed into the most extravagant and aromatic of confections.

There are a few points to note that will ensure perfect crêpes at every attempt. Do not make the batter too thick – it should be smooth and creamy. Do not over-beat the batter. Do not use too much batter for each crêpe. Do heat the pan thoroughly but do not over-grease it. Even the most expert chef may discard the first crêpe in a batch if the pan has not been prepared sufficiently – do not be discouraged!

Crêpes make quick desserts, and it is not essential to toss them. While some of us may have a natural flair or a burning desire to achieve this dramatic skill, it does not, in fact, make any difference to the finished product.

Batters made of white, wholemeal (whole wheat) and even buckwheat flour, leavened or not, are to be found in most countries. They were among the early recipes brought cross-country by the American pioneers. In Europe and Russia they were eaten with fresh or soured (sour) cream, fresh fruit or preserves. Thicker batters were used for fritters and baked puddings as well as for crêpes.

Crêpes also have well known Christian associations. Egg and dairy products were, of course, forbidden during Lent and so were used for a last binge during the celebration of Shrovetide which marked the end of winter. Shrove Tuesday, known popularly as Pancake Day, acquired its name as the last day of this feast period.

Today, restaurants or roadside stands selling pancakes, crêpes, *gauffres* and waffles abound all over the world. They are eaten for breakfast, brunch, dessert or simply as snacks. There is no end to the variations or the accompaniments – just a few of which are covered here!

PREPARATION

- ☛ Sift the flour and salt.
- ☛ Lightly beat the egg.
- ☛ Make a well in the centre of the flour and drop in the egg. Gradually beat the flour into the egg, adding the milk as the mixture gets too thick to stir easily.
- ☛ Whisk until smooth but do not over-beat.
- ☛ Use a heavy, shallow 18 cm/7 in frying pan to make the crêpes. Grease the pan just enough to give it a sheen and prevent the crêpes from sticking.
- ☛ Pour enough batter into the hot, greased pan to cover the bottom thinly.
- ☛ Cook the crêpe for approximately 1 minute, or until the under side is golden. Flip, and cook until the second side is golden.
- ☛ If the crêpes are not served immediately, stack and cover with a clean tea towel (napkin or dishcloth).

VARIATION

Stir finely grated rind of an orange or lemon into the batter.

For chocolate crêpes, add 1 tsp/5 g unsweetened cocoa.

You can also add 1 tbsp/15 ml liqueur of your choice for dessert crêpes.

Basic Crêpe Batter

INGREDIENTS

MAKES 8–10
1 cup + 2 tbsp/100 g/4 oz plain (all-purpose) flour
a pinch of salt
1 egg
1¼ cups/300 ml/½ pt milk

Crêpe Fillings

INGREDIENTS

SERVES 4—5

½ cup/100 g/4 oz pineapple pieces

1¼ cups/300 ml/10 oz Crème Pâtisserie
(see Cream Puffs, page 48)

4 tbsp/50 g/2 oz butter

2 tbsp/30 g icing (confectioners') sugar

PREPARATION

☞ Gently fold the pineapple pieces into the Crème Pâtisserie.

☞ Spread the filling mixture over the prepared crêpes. Fold the sides of the crêpe into the centre and place, seam side down, in a greased ovenproof serving dish.

☞ Melt the butter and brush over the surface of the filled crêpes.

☞ Sprinkle sifted sugar over the crêpes. Glaze quickly under a hot grill (broiler).

INGREDIENTS

1¼ cups/300 g/10 oz ice cream

1¼ cups/300 ml/10 oz fruit, butterscotch or
chocolate sauce

PREPARATION

☞ Place a scoop of ice cream on each crêpe. Fold the sides into the centre and place one or two on each person's plate.

☞ Pour warm sauce over the top and serve immediately.

INGREDIENTS

2 apples

1 tbsp/15 g/½ oz butter

2 tbsp/25 g/1 oz sugar

1–1⅓ cups/225 g/8 oz cream or curd (ricotta) cheese

PREPARATION

☞ Slice the apples and soften in melted butter. Stir in the brown sugar and continue cooking until the sugar has dissolved and the apple slices are well coated. Spoon carefully over each crêpe.

☞ Beat the cheese until it is smooth and spoon over the apples.

☞ Fold the crêpes and serve immediately.

Crêpes Suzette

INGREDIENTS

SERVES 8–10

2 tbsp/25 g/1 oz butter

¼ cup/50 g/2 oz sugar

2 oranges or tangerines

1 lemon

4 tbsp/60 ml Curaçao, Grand Marnier or Cointreau

PREPARATION

☛ Prepare the crêpes (see page 28).

☛ Melt the butter in a large frying pan.

☛ Stir in the sugar and continue to cook, stirring constantly, until the sugar has dissolved and the butter takes on a golden caramel colour. Stir the juice of the oranges or tangerines and half of the lemon into the caramel sauce. Continue to cook until the sauce comes to the boil and begins to thicken.

☛ Place one crêpe in the pan and gently stir so that it is coated with sauce. Fold into half, and half again, to make a triangular parcel.

☛ Push to the side of the pan to stay warm, and repeat the procedure with the remaining crêpes.

☛ When all the pancakes have been heated in the sauce, pour over the liqueur and flame. Serve as soon as the flames die down.

Strawberry Cheese Crêpes

INGREDIENTS

SERVES 4–5
1⅓ cups/225 g/8 oz strawberries, sliced
1⅓ cups/225 g/8 oz cottage cheese
1 tbsp/15 g/½ oz sugar
½ tsp/2½ g cinnamon
icing (confectioners') sugar

PREPARATION

☛ Prepare the crêpes (see page 28).
☛ Strain the cottage cheese and beat with the sugar and cinnamon until light and fluffy.
☛ Spread the cottage cheese over each crêpe and arrange strawberries on top.

TO SERVE

Fold and sprinkle with icing sugar.

VARIATION

Substitute peaches, apricots or any other soft fruit for the strawberries.
Dried fruit such as raisins, apricots, dates or figs can also be used. The fruit can be soaked in sherry, rum or wine for 1 hour before adding to the cheese.
As another alternative, try glacé (candied) fruit e.g. cherries, ginger or chestnuts.

Pancake Gâteau

INGREDIENTS

SERVES 8

CUSTARD

2 egg yolks

2 tbsp/25 g/1 oz sugar

½ cup/100 ml/4 fl oz double (heavy) cream

¼ tsp/2 ml vanilla essence (extract)

FRUIT PUREE

1½ cups/225 g/8 oz dried apricots

2½ cups/550 ml/1 pt water

¼ cup/50 g/2 oz sugar

oven temperature 180°C/350°F/Gas 4

PREPARATION

☛ Prepare the pancakes (see recipe page 28).

☛ Beat the egg yolks and sugar until they are very light. Add the cream and vanilla. Whisk until thick.

☛ Poach the apricots in water until they are tender. Drain, reserving the water. Purée the fruit and add sugar to taste. If necessary, thin the purée with the apricot juice.

☛ Grease a deep baking or soufflé dish. Alternate layers of pancakes and fruit purée ending with a pancake on top. Pour the custard mixture over the gâteau. Be sure that the custard goes down the sides of the dish so that all the layers are coated.

☛ Bake for 20 minutes.

☛ Place a serving dish over the top of the baking dish and flip over to invert the gâteau.

☛ Cool and serve plain or with a sauce of puréed fresh (or canned) apricots.

VARIATION

For an unbaked gâteau, spread a mixture of dried or diced fresh fruit and either cream cheese, curd cheese or strained cottage cheese between layers of pancakes on a pretty serving dish.

Blintzes

INGREDIENTS

SERVES 8—10

PANCAKES

3 eggs

1 cup + 2 tbsp/100 g/4 oz plain (all-purpose) flour

a pinch of salt

2 tsp/10 g sugar

1 cup/225 ml/8 fl oz milk

½ cup/100 ml/4 fl oz water

FILLING

2⅔ cups/450 g/1 lb cottage cheese

⅓ cup/75 g/3 oz sugar

¾ tsp/3 g cinnamon

PREPARATION

☛ For the pancakes, lightly beat the eggs.

☛ Sift the flour and stir in the salt and sugar.

☛ Stir the eggs, milk and water into the flour to make a smooth batter.

☛ Lightly grease a heavy 18 cm/7 in frying pan. Pour a spoonful of batter into the hot pan and tilt slightly to spread it over the base of the pan. Cook until the pancake has set. Do not turn the pancake but carefully slip it onto a clean dish cloth to cool. Repeat with all the mixture.

☛ Strain the cottage cheese and beat with the sugar and cinnamon until it is light and fluffy.

☛ Divide the cheese mixture evenly among the pancakes, spreading it over the cooked side of each one.

☛ Fold the pancakes over the filling into rectangular parcels.

☛ Fry the blintzes in melted butter until they are golden. Serve with natural yoghurt or soured (sour) cream and jam or puréed fruit.

VARIATION

1½ cups/350 g/12 oz cream cheese

⅓ cup/75 g/3 oz sugar

1 egg yolk

1 orange or lemon

PREPARATION

☛ Beat the cream cheese until it is soft. Add the sugar, egg yolk and finely grated rind of the orange or lemon. Beat until the cheese is light and fluffy.

☛ Assemble and cook the blintzes as above.

American Blueberry Pancakes

INGREDIENTS

SERVES 8–10
6¾ cups/675 g/1½ lb plain (all-purpose) flour
2 tbsp/30 g baking powder
1 tsp/5 g salt
2 eggs
¼ cup/50 g/2 oz butter or margarine
2 cups/450 ml/¾ pt milk
2–3 cups/450 g/1 lb blueberries
½ cup/100 ml/¼ pt water
¼ cup/50 g/2 oz sugar
1 piece of stick cinnamon
5 cm/2 in strip of lemon peel
2 tsp/10 g cornflour (cornstarch)

PREPARATION

☛ Sift the flour with the baking powder and salt.

☛ Lightly beat the eggs.

☛ Melt the butter or margarine.

☛ Make a well in the middle of the flour and pour in the eggs and butter. Stir the flour in gradually, drawing it from the edges towards the centre. As the batter becomes too thick to stir, begin adding the milk. Take care not to over-beat, but mix until the batter is smooth.

☛ Stir in half of the berries.

☛ Lightly grease the surface of a heavy frying pan. Spoon the batter in, making the pancakes as large or as small as you like. Cook until the surface is bubbly and the under side is golden. Flip the pancakes and cook until they are well risen and the bottom is golden.

☛ Place the water, sugar, cinnamon stick and lemon peel in a heavy based pan. Bring to the boil and cook over a high heat until the sugar has dissolved and the liquid is clear.

☛ Reduce the heat, add the fruit and simmer until the berries are soft.

☛ Sieve or liquidize the fruit.

☛ Mix the cornflour with just enough water to make a thick paste. Stir into the fruit purée. Return to the heat and cook, stirring constantly, until the sauce thickens.

☛ Stack the pancakes and spoon over the sauce.

Pastry

WALNUT CREAM TART   39

PECAN PIE   40

RASPBERRY COCONUT TART   41

DEEP DISH PUMPKIN PIE   43

NORMA'S DANISH   44

BAKLAVA   45

FRUIT STREUSEL PIE   47

CREAM PUFFS   48

APPLE STRUDEL   51

PUFF PASTRY   52

Opposite: Norma's Danish (see page 44)

Introduction

THERE WAS A TIME, a hundred or so years ago, when chefs throughout Europe, including Antonin Carême, used elaborate pastry constructions as the focal point of dinner tables. These creations, each more elaborate than the last, were placed on the table before the meal began and served an entirely decorative function. Pastry was to be admired for its appearance rather than its taste.

This, however, has not always been the case. Pies were one of the earliest American desserts, baked by the Pilgrims with pumpkin fillings, nuts and fruit from the harvest and often sweetened with maple syrup tapped from the trees abounding in the Colonies. At hoedowns, harvest home celebrations and house-raising parties, pies and cakes were the most popular desserts.

Puff pastry and choux pastry have been used for such tasty delights in France and Belgium that few people can walk past a pâtisserie without stopping to admire or buy. On a Sunday the queues (line-ups) outside the pastry shop before lunch include old and young, treating themselves to one of several classic desserts.

Further east, the *strudel* and *filo* pastries of the Balkans and the Middle East are famed for their flakiness and delicacy. Stretching *strudel* dough is an art form – experts may toss the pastry over their shoulders to pull it into transparent sheets. Mastering this technique is difficult and in Austria and Hungary it is taught virtually from childhood. *Filo,* a paper-thin dough popular in Greece, Tunisia and Turkey is baked in layers, filled with cream or nuts and soaked in syrup. The pastries of the Middle East are particularly sweet and sticky, intended as a suitable finale to a grand banquet.

Pastry, then, is loved by many and used for family meals and feasts alike. It can lend substance and style to your table. These recipes, taken from many sources, are intended as an introduction to the many varieties.

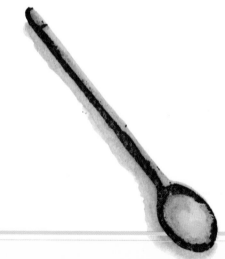

Walnut Cream Tart

PREPARATION

☛ Roll out the pastry and line the base and sides of a 20 cm/8 in pie flan dish (straight-sided pie plate).

☛ Spread the jam over the pastry.

☛ Combine the walnuts, rum, cream and vanilla essence in a liquidizer or food processor until they are smooth.

☛ Beat the egg yolks with the sugar until they are thick and nearly white. Stir into the nut mixture.

☛ Whisk the egg whites until they are stiff but not dry. Gently fold into the nut mixture, starting with just one spoonful and gradually adding the remainder.

☛ Pour the filling into the pastry case (pie shell) and bake for 30 minutes or until firm. Leave to cool.

☛ Beat the egg yolks for the topping with the sugar until they are thick and nearly white.

☛ Soak the gelatine in cold water, then dissolve in the brandy over a very low heat. If you are using powdered gelatine, warm the brandy, sprinkle in the gelatine and stir until it has dissolved.

☛ Stir the gelatine into the egg yolks.

☛ Whisk the cream until it is just firm enough to hold its shape. Fold into the egg mixture.

☛ Whisk the egg whites until they are stiff but not dry. Gently fold into the cream and egg mixture, starting with just one spoonful and gradually adding the remainder.

☛ Tie a 10 cm/4 in collar of greaseproof (waxed) paper around the outside of the baked flan. Carefully pour the topping mixture over the flan. Leave in the refrigerator to set for several hours.

☛ Sprinkle the walnuts over the top of the tart just as it begins to set.

INGREDIENTS

SERVES 10–12

BASE

½ lb/225 g/8 oz sweet shortcrust pastry (basic pie dough)

2 tbsp/30 g apricot jam

FILLING

1½ cups/175 g/6 oz walnuts

4 tbsp/60 ml dark rum

2 tbsp/30 ml double (heavy) cream

1 tsp/5 ml vanilla essence (extract)

3 eggs, separated

¾ cup/175 g/6 oz sugar

oven temperature 190°C/375°F/Gas 5

TOPPING

2 eggs, separated

⅓ cup/75 g/3 oz sugar

3 leaves of gelatine (gelatin)

¼ cup/50 ml/2 fl oz brandy

2 cups/450 ml/¾ pt whipping cream

½ cup/50 g/2 oz walnuts, coarsely chopped

Pecan Pie

INGREDIENTS

SERVES 6–8

PASTRY

4 tbsp/50 g/2 oz margarine

1 cup + 2 tbsp/100 g/4 oz plain (all-purpose) flour

a pinch of salt

3 tbsp/45 ml cold water

FILLING

2 eggs

½ tsp/2½ ml vanilla essence (extract)

½ cup/100 g/4 oz light brown sugar

3 tbsp/45 g/1½ oz butter

¼ cup/50 ml/2 fl oz golden (light corn) syrup

a pinch of salt

1 cup/100 g/4 oz pecans, chopped

oven temperature 200°C/400°F/Gas 6
and 160°C/300°F/Gas 2

PREPARATION

☛ Rub the margarine into the sifted flour and salt until the mixture resembles coarse breadcrumbs. Bind with the water, adding it one spoonful at a time to ensure that the dough doesn't get sticky.

☛ Roll out the dough to line a 20 cm/8 in flan dish or shallow pie plate.

☛ Chill the pastry while you prepare the filling.

☛ Lightly beat the eggs with the vanilla essence. Add the sugar and mix well.

☛ Stir in the melted butter, golden syrup and salt. Mix until well blended. Stir in the pecans, reserving a few for decoration.

☛ Pour the filling into the pastry case, arrange the reserved pecans in an attractive pattern on top and bake for 10 minutes at the higher temperature. Reduce the temperature and continue baking for 20 minutes or until the filling has set. Leave to cool.

TO SERVE

Accompany with pouring or whipped cream, or ice cream.

Raspberry Coconut Tart

INGREDIENTS

SERVES 6

PASTRY

4 tbsp/50 g/2 oz butter

4 tbsp/50 g/2 oz margarine

1½ cups/175 g/6 oz plain (all-purpose) flour

1 egg

oven temperature 220°C/425°F/Gas 7

FILLING

2 tbsp/30 g raspberry jam

½ cup/100 g/4 oz soft margarine

⅓ cup/75 g/3 oz sugar

1 cup + 2 tbsp/100 g/4 oz plain (all-purpose) flour

1 tsp/5 g baking powder

2 eggs

1 tsp/5 ml almond essence

¼ cup/50 g/2 oz desiccated (shredded) coconut

oven temperature 180°C/350°F/Gas 4

PREPARATION

☛ Rub the butter and margarine into the flour until the mixture resembles coarse breadcrumbs. Bind with the lightly beaten egg. Chill for 1 hour, and then roll out and line a 20 cm/8 in loose-bottomed pie dish or cake pan.

☛ Bake the pastry for 5 minutes.

☛ Cool slightly and spread with raspberry jam.

☛ Beat the soft margarine with the sugar, flour and baking powder until smooth. Add the eggs and almond essence. Mix well. Stir in the coconut.

☛ Pour the filling into the pastry case (shell) and bake for 20 minutes. Cool before serving.

Deep Dish Pumpkin Pie

INGREDIENTS

SERVES 8–10
PASTRY
6 tbsp/75 ml/3 oz vegetable fat (shortening)
2³/₄ cups/300 g/10 oz plain (all-purpose) flour
½ tsp/2½ g salt
¼ cup/50 ml/2 fl oz water
FILLING
2 cups/450 g/1 lb pumpkin purée
½ cup/100 g/4 oz brown sugar
3 eggs
1 tsp/5 g cinnamon
½ tsp/2½ g ground ginger
½ tsp/2½ g ground cloves
½ tsp/2½ g nutmeg
½ tsp/2½ g salt
¼ cup/50 ml/2 fl oz sweet sherry
1¼ cups/300 ml/½ pt double (heavy) cream
1 cup/225 ml/8 fl oz milk

oven temperature 180°C/350°F/Gas 4

PREPARATION

☛ Rub the fat into the sifted flour and salt until the mixture resembles coarse breadcrumbs. Bind with the water, adding it a spoonful at a time so that the dough isn't too sticky.

☛ Roll out the pastry to line a deep 23 cm/9 in pie dish. Make sure that the top of the pastry comes 2½ cm/1 in above the top of the dish. Chill the pastry case (shell) while you mix the filling.

☛ Beat the pumpkin purée with the sugar until smooth.

☛ Add the lightly whisked eggs and all the spices. Mix well.

☛ Stir in the sherry, cream and milk.

☛ Place the pie dish on a baking sheet to catch any overflow. Carefully pour the filling into the pastry case (shell).

☛ Bake for 1¼ hours or until the filling has set. Cool in the oven with the door slightly open as the filling drops while it cools. If it drops too suddenly, cracks will appear in the surface.

☛ Chill the pie and serve with pouring or whipped cream.

Norma's Danish

INGREDIENTS

MAKES 24

PASTRY

1 cup/225 g/8 oz margarine

2¼ cups/225 g/8 oz self-raising (self-rising) flour

1 cup/225 g/8 oz curd (ricotta) cheese

FILLING

½ cup/100 g/4 oz jam OR

⅔ cup/100 g/4 oz raisins, sultanas (white raisins) and glacé (candied) cherries or chopped nuts

oven temperature 180°C/350°F/Gas 4

ICING

¾ cup/100 g/4 oz icing (confectioners') sugar

1–2 tbsp/15–30 ml lemon juice

PREPARATION

☛ Rub the margarine into the flour until the mixture resembles coarse breadcrumbs. Add the cheese and mix well to form a soft dough. Wrap in foil and chill for 1 hour.

☛ Unwrap and knead the dough in a little bit of flour so that it is smooth and not sticky. Roll out to make a large rectangle.

☛ Spread the jam over the surface or sprinkle with fruit and nuts. Roll as for a Swiss (jelly) roll. Seal well. Cut into slices approximately 2½ cm/1 in thick. Place the pastries on a greased baking sheet cut side up. Bake for 20 minutes or until firm and golden.

☛ Sift the icing sugar and stir in the lemon juice to make a thick icing. Spread over the pastries while they are still warm.

Baklava

INGREDIENTS

SERVES 8-12

1 cup/225 g/8 oz sugar

²/₃ cup/150 ml/¹/₄ pt water

1 tbsp/15 ml lemon juice

1 cup/225 g/8 oz butter, melted

24 sheets filo (phyllo) pastry

1¹/₃ cups/225 g/8 oz chopped nuts

*oven temperature 180°C/350°F/Gas 4 and
230°C/450°F/Gas 8*

PREPARATION

☛ Place the sugar, water and lemon juice in a heavy-bottomed pan. Heat, stirring constantly, until the sugar has dissolved. Increase the heat and boil the syrup for 5 minutes. Leave to cool.

☛ Brush melted butter over the base and sides of a 23 × 28 cm/9 × 11 in roasting pan.

☛ Arrange a layer of pastry over the base of the pan, overlapping to cover the entire surface. Brush with butter and sprinkle with nuts.

☛ Cover with another layer of pastry and repeat the process until you have used all the nuts and pastry. Brush each layer of pastry well with the butter and finish with a layer of pastry.

☛ Cut into diamond-shaped pieces. Bake for 30 minutes at the lower temperature and then increase for another 15 minutes or until golden. Pour over the syrup and leave to cool before serving.

Fruit Streusel Pie

INGREDIENTS

SERVES 8
PASTRY
1½ cups/175 g/6 oz plain (all-purpose) flour
¾ tsp/4 g baking powder
a pinch of salt
2 tbsp/25 g/1 oz sugar
½ cup/100 g/4 oz butter or margarine
1 egg
1 tbsp/15 ml milk
FILLING
¼ cup/50 g/2 oz sugar
1 tsp/5 g cornflour (cornstarch)
½ tsp/2½ g cinnamon
1½ cups/350 g/12 oz fruit of your choice
2 tbsp/30 ml water
TOPPING
½ cup/50 g/2 oz plain (all-purpose) flour
1 tbsp/15 g sugar
1 tsp/5 g cinnamon
2 tbsp/25 g/1 oz butter

oven temperature 200°C/400°F/Gas 6

PREPARATION

☛ Combine all the dry ingredients for the pastry. Rub in the butter or margarine until the mixture resembles coarse breadcrumbs. Bind into a dough with the lightly beaten egg and milk.

☛ The pastry will be too soft to roll, so work carefully with the tips of your fingers and press the pastry over the base and sides of a 23 cm/9 in deep pie dish.

☛ Combine the sugar, cornflour and cinnamon for the filling. Add to the fruit, along with the water, and mix well.

☛ Spread the fruit filling in the pastry case (shell).

☛ Combine the dry ingredients for the topping and rub in the butter until the mixture resembles coarse breadcrumbs. Sprinkle over the fruit filling.

☛ Bake the pie for 40 minutes or until the pastry is golden.

TO SERVE

Serve warm or cold, accompanied by cream or ice cream.

Cream Puffs

INGREDIENTS

MAKES 24

CHOUX PASTRY

²/₃ cup/65 g/2¹/₂ oz plain (all-purpose) flour

a pinch of salt

4 tbsp/50 g/2 oz butter

²/₃ cup/150 ml/¹/₄ pt water

2 eggs

oven temperature 220°C/425°F/Gas 7

CREME PATISSERIE

3 tbsp/45 ml/1¹/₂ oz sugar

2 tsp/10 g cornflour (cornstarch)

1 tbsp/15 g plain (all-purpose) flour

2 eggs

1¹/₄ cups/300 ml/¹/₂ pt milk

PREPARATION

☞ Sift the flour and salt.

☞ Heat the butter and water together until the butter has melted and the water is just about to boil.

☞ Add the flour and stir with a wooden spoon until the mixture forms a ball which leaves the sides of the pan clean. Remove from the heat and leave to cool for 2–3 minutes.

☞ Lightly beat the eggs and stir into the dough. Mix well. It should be just firm enough to hold its shape.

☞ Drop small spoonfuls of dough onto a greased baking sheet and bake for 15 minutes or until well risen and golden brown. Transfer to a wire rack to cool.

☞ Combine the sugar, cornflour and flour. Add one whole egg plus the yolk of the second and mix well.

☞ Heat the milk until it is just about to boil. Pour over the egg mixture and blend well. Return to the pan and cook over a low heat, stirring constantly, until thick.

☞ Leave to cool, stirring occasionally, to prevent a skin forming.

☞ To assemble the cream puffs, cut the choux buns nearly in half and place a spoonful of filling in each.

TO SERVE

Sprinkle with icing (confectioners') sugar or spread with chocolate icing. Serve immediately.

VARIATION

To make eclairs, pipe the choux pastry onto baking sheets in 8 cm/3 in lengths. Bake for 20 minutes then cool and fill as above.

To make profiteroles, pile cream puffs in a pyramid and pour chocolate sauce over the top.

Apple Strudel

INGREDIENTS

SERVES 8–10

PASTRY

2¼ cups/225 g/8 oz bread (hard wheat) flour

1 small egg

1 tsp/5 g sugar

a pinch of salt

1 tbsp/15 ml melted butter or oil

¼ cup/50 ml/2 fl oz warm water

FILLING

½ cup/50 g/2 oz breadcrumbs

4 tbsp/50 g/2 oz butter

1 lb/450 g cooking apples, peeled and thinly sliced

⅓ cup/75 g/3 oz sugar

⅓ cup/50 g/2 oz sultanas (white raisins)

⅓ cup/50 g/2 oz chopped almonds or hazelnuts (filberts)

oven temperature 190°C/375°F/Gas 5

PREPARATION

☛ Place the flour in a large mixing bowl and make a well in the centre. Add the lightly beaten egg, sugar, salt, and butter or oil. Gradually draw the flour into the centre to make the dough.

☛ Gradually add the water to make a soft, sticky dough. Knead the dough until it is smooth and no longer sticky.

☛ Leave the dough to rest for 30 minutes, covered with a bowl or clean cloth.

☛ Sprinkle a cloth-covered table with flour and roll the dough out very thinly to a large circle. Lightly brush with oil or melted butter.

☛ Lift and stretch gently until nearly transparent. Trim off any edges that may still be thick or hard.

☛ Brush the centre of the pastry with melted butter, leaving a margin of approximately 2½ cm/1 in all the way around.

☛ Brown the breadcrumbs in melted butter and sprinkle over the strudel pastry.

☛ Arrange the apples over the breadcrumbs and sprinkle with sugar. Scatter the sultanas and nuts over the top.

☛ Fold the top, bottom and one long side of the pastry over the filling. Brush the fourth side with melted butter and place a sheet of greaseproof (waxed) paper under it.

☛ Roll the strudel towards the unfolded edge. Lift the paper onto a greased baking sheet.

☛ Brush the surface with melted butter and bake for 30 minutes or until the pastry is crisp and golden.

☛ Serve the strudel warm, sprinkled with icing (confectioners') sugar and accompanied by a bowl of cream.

VARIATION

½ cup/50 g/2 oz fresh breadcrumbs

½ cup/100 g/4 oz butter

3 tbsp/45 g ground almonds

⅓ cup/50 g/2 oz sultanas (white raisins)

¼ cup/50 g/2 oz sugar

1 cup/225 g/8 oz curd (ricotta) cheese

1 egg

½ lemon

PREPARATION

☛ Brown the breadcrumbs in half of the butter and sprinkle over the strudel pastry.

☛ Sprinkle the ground almonds and sultanas over the crumbs.

☛ Cream the remaining butter with the sugar until light and fluffy. Add the cheese, egg yolk and grated rind and juice of the lemon. Beat well.

☛ Whisk the egg white until it is stiff but not dry. Gently fold into the cheese mixture, starting with just one spoonful and gradually adding the remainder.

☛ Spread the cheese filling on top of the crumbs and fruit.

☛ Fold and bake the strudel as described above.

Puff Pastry

INGREDIENTS

4½ cups/450 g/1 lb plain (all-purpose) flour

2 tsp/10 g salt

2 tsp/10 ml lemon juice

2 cups/450 g/1 lb butter, cut into small cubes and softened

1¼ cups/300 ml/½ pt water

oven temperature 230°C/450°F/Gas 8

PREPARATION

☛ Sift the flour and salt into a large bowl. Make a well in the centre and add the lemon juice, water and ¼ of the butter.

☛ Gradually draw the flour into the centre and knead lightly, until the dough is smooth. Shape into a ball, wrap in cling film (plastic wrap) and chill for 15 minutes.

☛ Roll the dough out to make a thick 30 cm/12 in square. Place the remaining butter in the centre. Fold the dough around the butter.

☛ Place the dough, seam side down, on a floured surface. Press down gently with the rolling pin.

☛ Roll out the dough to make a large rectangle, approximately 20 × 40 cm/8 × 16 in.

☛ Fold the rectangle in thirds by folding first the bottom third and then the top third into the middle. Gently seal the folds with the rolling pin and turn in a quarter circle so the folds are in the other direction, roll, fold and seal again. Wrap the dough once more and chill for 15 minutes.

☛ Repeat this procedure twice.

☛ Roll out and fill the pastry (see below). Glaze with a lightly beaten egg, sprinkle with sugar and bake in a preheated oven until well risen and golden.

Fillings

MILLE FEUILLES

☛ Roll puff pastry out to make a large rectangle, approximately 23 × 25 cm/9 × 10 in. Prick the surface with a fork and bake on a damp baking sheet for 20 minutes or until well risen and golden.

☛ Cool, then cut the pastry through the centre to make two layers.

☛ Spread the bottom layer with whipped cream and sprinkle with blackberries, raspberries or strawberries. Alternatively, spread with jam and then cream.

☛ Cover with the top layer of pastry.

☛ Make glacé icing. Mix one spoonful with a few drops of red food colouring. Spread the white icing over the top and then pipe thin lines of pink icing across the surface. Use the tip of a knife to draw the icing across the width of the pastry giving a feathered effect.

JALOUSIE

☛ Roll puff pastry out to make a large rectangle. Cut in half lengthways. Spread one piece of pastry with jam or sliced apples cooked in butter and sprinkled with sugar. Leave 1 cm/½ in clear on all sides.

☛ Brush the edges with cold water.

☛ Fold the remaining rectangle of pastry in half length ways. Make cuts in the pastry from the folded edge almost to the outside edge at intervals of 1 cm/½ in.

☛ Place the cut pastry on top of the filling. Carefully unfold the top piece of pastry and seal well around all the edges. Brush with lightly beaten egg and sprinkle with sugar.

☛ Bake for 30 minutes or until well risen and golden.

TURNOVERS

☛ Roll puff pastry out to make a large square. Cut into smaller squares.

☛ Place a spoonful of jam, cooked fruit or marzipan (almond paste) in the centre of each square.

☛ Brush the edges of the pastry with water and fold to make a triangle. Seal well. Brush with lightly beaten egg, sprinkle with sugar and bake until well risen and golden.

Opposite: Jalousie

Fruit

ORANGE DREAM   57

HOT FRUIT SALAD   58

STUFFED PEACHES   59

CARAMEL ORANGES   60

GINGERED PEACHES   61

APPLE CREAM   63

FROZEN LEMON MOUSSE   64

FRUIT MERINGUE   65

BLACKBERRY MERINGUE TRIFLE   66

GOOSEBERRY ROULADE   67

STRAWBERRY SHORTCAKE   68

BAKED BANANAS   70

BAKED PINEAPPLE RINGS   71

Introduction

HICH CAME FIRST, the sweet tooth or the sweet? Did the first dessert eaters seek out sugar or did they find it in the fruit of the earth and shout 'Eureka!'?

Fruit must surely have been Man's first dessert. It was readily available and a tempting introduction to sweets as Eve knew, only too well. Fruit remains one of our favourite foods, fresh and succulent or preserved by drying, freezing and canning. It is widely distributed around the world, not least because people migrating across countries and even continents took seeds, cuttings and recipes wherever they travelled. We now cultivate our fruit assiduously. If all other sources of sugar were to disappear, we would still have no shortage of desserts.

The miracles of transportation make fresh fruit available the year round, imported from every point on earth to virtually everywhere it is in demand. Seasons are of little consequence. Recipes can be truly international.

What, then, do we do with fruit? A basket or crystal dish piled high with a selection of fruit may tempt even the most replete diner. Is there no end to the creation of fruit salads to finish a meal? We make compotes to serve warm on a dark, cold winter's night. We make ices to cool on a summer's eve. We make purées to blend with cream or cheese. We peel and chop, preserve in syrup or alcohol all manner of fruit. We have eaten fruit for dessert for centuries and almost certainly will continue to do so for centuries to come.

Orange Dream

SERVES 4

2 oranges

1 cup/225 g/8 oz cream cheese (mascarpone if possible)

2 tsp/10 g icing (confectioners') sugar

2 tsp/10 ml Cointreau or Curaçao

¼ cup/50 g/2 oz biscuit (cookie) crumbs

PREPARATION

☛ Peel and thinly slice the oranges. Arrange in the bottom of one large or four small serving dishes.
☛ Beat the cheese until it is smooth. Sweeten with sifted icing (confectioners') sugar. Stir in the liqueur.
☛ Spoon or pipe the cheese onto the fruit.
☛ Top with crushed biscuits.
☛ Chill for 30 minutes before serving.

VARIATION

Vary the fruit and liqueur according to taste eg cherries and kirsch, blackcurrants and cassis.
Alternatively, soak some raisins or figs in sherry or brandy and mix into the cheese.
Garnish the dessert with pieces of whole fruit, candied peel or grated chocolate.

Hot Fruit Salad

INGREDIENTS

SERVES 4

2½ cups/450 g/1 lb dried fruit eg apricots, raisins, figs

¼ cup/50 g/2 oz brown sugar

1 piece of stick cinnamon

2 tsp/10 ml lemon juice

PREPARATION

☛ Cover the dried fruit with water and leave to soak overnight.

☛ Drain the fruit and combine the liquid with the brown sugar, cinnamon stick and lemon juice. Heat, stirring constantly, until the sugar has dissolved and then boil for 10 minutes or until the syrup begins to thicken.

☛ Add the fruit to the syrup and poach gently for 30 minutes or until the fruit is soft. Serve immediately.

VARIATION

2½ cups/450 g/1 lb dried fruit

¼ cup/50 g/2 oz sugar

orange or rose flower water

¾ cup/125 g/4 oz nuts, almonds or pistachios

PREPARATION

☛ Cover the fruit with water as above and add the sugar. Stir in the orange or rose flower water and add the nuts. Do not cook but leave the fruit to soak for 2–3 days. Heat gently before serving.

Stuffed Peaches

INGREDIENTS

SERVES 4

4 peaches, stoned and halved

4 tbsp/60 g macaroon crumbs

2 tbsp/30 g glacé (candied) cherries, finely chopped

8 blanched almonds

Marsala, Muscatel or sweet white wine

oven temperature 180°C/350°F/Gas 4

PREPARATION

☞ Remove some of the peach pulp, but make sure to leave enough to keep the fruit firm.

☞ Mash the pulp and mix with the macaroon crumbs and cherries.

☞ Pile the filling into the peach halves. Top each with an almond.

☞ Arrange the peaches in a well greased, shallow ovenproof dish. Sprinkle with the wine.

☞ Bake for 20–30 minutes. Serve hot or cold.

Caramel Oranges

INGREDIENTS

SERVES 6

6 medium oranges

3³/4 cups/850 ml/1¹/2 pt water

3 cups/675 g/1¹/2 lb sugar

PREPARATION

☛ Cut the skin of the oranges into thin strips and boil in water for 2 minutes. Drain well. Repeat this process twice, with fresh water each time to remove the bitterness.

☛ Thinly slice the oranges and arrange in a serving dish.

☛ Heat the sugar with the water until the sugar has dissolved. Bring the syrup to the boil and cook for 15 minutes. Pour over the oranges and leave to stand for 2–3 hours.

☛ Drain the syrup off the oranges and boil for another 15 minutes. Scatter the peel over the oranges, pour on the syrup and leave to cool. Chill for at least 8 hours before serving with fresh cream or ice cream.

VARIATION

6 medium oranges, unpeeled and sliced

1¹/2 cups/350 g/12 oz sugar

15 cloves

1 piece of stick cinnamon

¹/3 cup/75 ml/3 fl oz wine vinegar

PREPARATION

☛ Cover the oranges with cold water and bring to the boil. Simmer for 30 minutes and drain.

☛ Combine the remaining ingredients. Heat, stirring continuously, until the sugar has dissolved and then boil for 5 minutes.

☛ Poach the oranges, a few slices at a time, until they are transparent.

☛ When all the fruit has been cooked, pour the syrup over it. Leave to stand for at least 2–3 hours.

☛ Drain the syrup off the oranges and boil rapidly until it begins to thicken. Return the oranges to the pan and heat through if you want to serve them warm, or just pour the syrup over the fruit and leave to cool if you want to serve chilled. Serve with cream or ice cream.

Gingered Peaches

INGREDIENTS

SERVES 4

4 peaches

4 tbsp/50 g/2 oz butter

2 tbsp/30 g brown sugar

¼ cup/50 g/2 oz stem ginger in syrup, diced

2 tbsp/30 ml rum or brandy

PREPARATION

☛ Plunge the peaches into boiling water for 1 minute. Remove and peel off skins. Slice thinly.
☛ Melt the butter and stir in the sugar until it has dissolved. Add the ginger and arrange the peach slices in the butter. Heat gently, turning and basting frequently.

TO SERVE

Serve hot with cream or ice cream and home-made biscuits (cookies).

To flame the fruit, warm the rum or brandy in a ladle. Pour over the fruit and set alight. Serve as soon as the flames have died down.

Apple Cream

INGREDIENTS

SERVES 8

1 lb/450 g apples, sliced with their skins

juice of 1 orange

2 tbsp/30 ml white wine

2 tsp/10 ml orange or rose flower water

½ cup/100 g/4 oz butter

1¼ cups/300 ml/½ pt double (heavy) cream

PREPARATION

☞ Place the apples in a heavy-bottomed pan with the juice of the orange and the white wine. Cook on a low heat until the apples are tender. Cool slightly and purée. Stir the orange or rose flower water into the purée.

☞ Soften the butter and beat into the apple purée until smooth and well blended.

☞ Whisk the cream until it is just beginning to thicken. Gently fold into the purée.

☞ Turn the apple cream into serving dishes and chill for at least 4 hours or until it is firm.

☞ Serve the apple cream with plain biscuits (cookies) or with poached apple slices.

Frozen Lemon Mousse

INGREDIENTS

SERVES 6

2 eggs, separated

¼ cup/50 g/2 oz sugar

juice and finely grated rind of 1 lemon

1¼ cups/300 ml/½ pt double (heavy) cream

¾ cup/75 g/3 oz biscuit (cookie) crumbs

PREPARATION

☛ Whisk the egg yolks, gradually adding the sugar, until thick and nearly white.

☛ Beat in the lemon juice and rind.

☛ Lightly whip the cream and gently stir into the egg.

☛ Whisk the egg whites until they are stiff but not dry. Carefully fold into the mousse, starting with just one spoonful and gradually adding the remainder.

☛ Sprinkle half of the biscuit crumbs over the base of a 1 lb/450 g loaf pan. Pour in the mousse. Top with the remaining crumbs.

☛ Freeze the mousse for at least 8 hours.

☛ Remove from the freezer 30 minutes before serving.

Fruit Meringue

INGREDIENTS

SERVES 8

6 egg whites

1½ cups/350 g/12 oz sugar

2 lb/900 g fruit eg plums, pears, sliced

2½ cups/550 ml/1 pt water or red wine

½ cup/100 g/4 oz sugar

1¼ cups/300 ml/½ pt double (heavy) cream

¼ cup/50 g/2 oz chopped nuts

oven temperature 170°C/325°F/Gas 3

PREPARATION

☞ To make the meringues, whisk the egg whites until they are very stiff. Gradually fold in the sugar.
☞ Line two flat baking trays with greaseproof (waxed) paper. Draw a large circle on each. Spoon or pipe the meringue onto the circle and spread evenly. Bake for 1 hour.
☞ Turn off the oven and leave the door slightly open until the meringues have cooled completely. Turn one of the meringues, upside down, onto a large serving dish.
☞ Poach the fruit in water or wine. When the fruit is soft, drain well and remove skins. Liquidize the fruit and sweeten to taste.
☞ If you have cooked the fruit in water, brandy or liqueur can be added to the purée.
☞ Spread the fruit carefully over the meringue base.
☞ Lightly whip the cream and spread half over the fruit.
☞ Gently place the second meringue on top of the cream.
☞ Decorate with the remaining cream and sprinkle with chopped nuts.

VARIATION

Ground almonds, hazelnuts, unsweetened cocoa or instant coffee granules can be added to the egg whites for the meringue.

Blackberry Meringue Trifle

INGREDIENTS

SERVES 8

18 sponge fingers (Boudoir biscuits)

juice of 1 orange

1½ cups/225 g/8 oz blackberries

2½ cups/550 ml/1 pt custard, warm

3 egg whites

1 tbsp/15 g sugar

oven temperature 220°C/425°F/Gas 7

PREPARATION

☛ Arrange the sponge fingers in the bottom of a deep glass serving dish. Sprinkle with the orange juice.
☛ Arrange the fruit over the top of the sponge.
☛ Pour the custard over the fruit and leave to set.
☛ Whisk the egg whites until they are stiff but not dry. Carefully fold in the sugar.
☛ Spoon the meringue over the custard, ensuring that it comes right to the edge of the dish.
☛ Bake the trifle for 10 minutes or until the meringue is just beginning to brown. Cool and chill before serving.

VARIATION

Try this trifle with any other fresh, canned or frozen fruit available.

Gooseberry Roulade

INGREDIENTS

SERVES 4
3 eggs
6 tbsp/75 g/3 oz sugar
1 cup + 2 tbsp/100 g/4 oz plain (all-purpose) flour
1½ cups/225 g/8 oz gooseberries
¼ cup/50 ml/2 fl oz water
¼ cup/50 g/2 oz sugar
2 tsp/10 g arrowroot

oven temperature 220°C/425°F/Gas 7

PREPARATION

☛ Whisk the eggs and sugar until they are light and frothy. Gently fold in the sifted flour.

☛ Grease and line a Swiss (jelly) roll pan with greaseproof (waxed) paper. Pour in the roulade mixture, tilting the pan slightly to make sure that the corners are filled.

☛ Bake for 10 minutes or until firm to the touch.

☛ Turn the roulade out of the pan onto a clean piece of paper.

☛ Poach the gooseberries in water until they are tender. Drain well but save the cooking liquid.

☛ Purée the fruit and stir in sugar to taste. Cool slightly.

☛ Spread the gooseberry purée over the roulade. Roll lengthways and lift carefully onto a serving dish.

☛ To make the sauce, heat the liquid from the gooseberries until it is boiling.

☛ Mix the arrowroot with a little bit of water and stir into the hot juice. Continue to cook, stirring constantly, until the sauce thickens. Pour some over the roulade and serve the rest separately.

Strawberry Shortcake

INGREDIENTS

SERVES 8

2½ cups/450 g/1 lb strawberries

¼ cup/50 g/2 oz sugar

2¼ cups/225 g/8 oz plain (all-purpose) flour

4 tsp/20 g baking powder

½ tsp/2½ g salt

1 tbsp/15 g/½ oz sugar

6 tbsp/75 g/3 oz butter

½ cup/100 ml/4 fl oz milk

1¼ cups/300 ml/½ pt double (heavy) cream

oven temperature 220°C/425°F/Gas 7

PREPARATION

☞ Set aside enough strawberries to decorate the top of the shortcake and slice the remainder. Sprinkle with some of the sugar, mix gently, and leave for 1 hour.

☞ Sift the flour, baking powder and salt. Stir in the remaining sugar. Rub in 4 tbsp/50 g/2 oz butter so that the mixture resembles coarse breadcrumbs. Bind to a dough with the milk.

☞ Knead the dough very lightly so that it is smooth, and cut in half. Roll each piece into a round 23 cm/9 in in diameter. Place one round on a flat baking tray.

☞ Melt the remaining butter and brush over the surface of the shortcake which is on the baking tray. Carefully place the second round on top of it. Bake for 12 minutes or until golden. Leave to cool slightly.

☞ While the shortcake is still warm, gently split the layers.

☞ Lightly whip the cream and spread ¾ over the bottom layer of shortbread. Arrange the sliced fruit over the cream and top with the second layer of shortbread.

☞ Spread the remaining cream over the top layer and decorate with the whole strawberries. Serve warm or chilled.

VARIATION

Substitute any other available fruit for the strawberries eg blackberries, raspberries, blueberries, peaches, pineapple etc. A mixed fruit shortcake is also delicious and can be a beautiful centrepiece.

Baked Bananas

INGREDIENTS

SERVES 4

4 bananas, peeled

4 tsp/20 g butter

4 tsp/20 g dark brown sugar

4 tsp/20 ml rum

oven temperature 200°C/400°F/Gas 6

PREPARATION

☞ Place the bananas on a large square of foil. Dot each banana with a spoonful of butter.
☞ Sprinkle each with a spoonful of sugar and rum.
☞ Fold the foil not too tightly but well sealed. Bake for 15 minutes.

TO SERVE

Unwrap each banana and arrange on a serving dish. Top with a scoop of ice cream.

VARIATION

Bake or barbecue the bananas in their skins and let everyone pour on their own rum.

Alternatively, scatter chocolate buttons (drops) over them before wrapping in foil.

Baked Pineapple Rings

INGREDIENTS

SERVES 8

1 large pineapple, sliced in 8 rings

4 tbsp/60 g apricot jam (preserves)

2 tbsp/30 ml kirsch (optional)

oven temperature 200°C/400°F/Gas 6

PREPARATION

☛ Arrange the pineapple rings on a large baking tray. Spread with apricot jam and sprinkle over the kirsch.
☛ Bake for 5–10 minutes.

VARIATION

☛ As with Baked Bananas (see page 70), pineapple rings can be cooked to perfection on a barbecue. In this case, spread both sides of the pineapple with jam and grill for 3–4 minutes on each side.

Chocolate

TRUFFLES	75
CHERRY CHOCOLATE CRUNCH	76
CHOC NUT SLICE	77
RED VELVET CAKE	78
CHOCOLATE CHIP CAKE	79
CHOCOLATE RUM CAKE	80
BROWNIES	81
FLORENTINES	82
CHOCOLATE FONDUE	83
CHOCOLATE ORANGE MOUSSE	84
CHESTNUT MOUSSE	85
CHOCOLATE CRISPIES	87

Opposite: Truffles (see page 75)

Introduction

CHOCOLATE is known as the devil's food for good reason. There is nothing more wicked, sinful or luxurious than a chocolate dessert. It can be chewy or gooey, crunchy or crispy, thoroughly chocolate or tantalizingly garnished with chocolate.

Homemade chocolate desserts are among the most extravagant any good cook can prepare. They can vary from fruit or cake dipped into chocolate sauce, to the richest mousse or the lightest soufflé. Sacher Torte and Black Forest Gâteau offer luxury beyond compare. Profiteroles and éclairs, truffles and fudge, chocolate frostings and *chiffon* pies, hot puddings and ice cream, tempt even the strong hearted. But there is, indeed, enjoyment of anything chocolate and this chapter is meant especially for those who feel they can cope with the stress!

Truffles

INGREDIENTS

MAKES 12

½ cup/100 g/4 oz plain (dark) chocolate in small pieces

3 tbsp/45 ml single (light) cream

½ cup/100 g/4 oz ground almonds

2 tbsp/30 ml rum or brandy

2 cups/225 g/8 oz biscuit (cookie) or cake crumbs

¾ cup/100 g/4 oz icing sugar (confectioners') sugar OR
¼ cup/50 g/2 oz chocolate strands

PREPARATION

☞ Melt the chocolate in the top of a double boiler.
☞ Pour the chocolate into a mixing bowl with the cream, ground almonds, rum or brandy and crumbs.
☞ Mix well and chill for 1 hour, or until it is firm enough to handle.
☞ Divide the chocolate mixture into 12 pieces. Roll into small balls and toss in sifted sugar or chocolate strands.

VARIATION

---

1 cup/225 g/8 oz plain chocolate in small pieces

2 tbsp/30 g butter

2 egg yolks

2 tsp/10 ml single cream

¾ cup/100 g/4 oz icing sugar OR
¼ cup/50 g/2 oz chocolate strands

PREPARATION

☞ Melt the chocolate as above.
☞ Mix with the softened butter, yolks and cream.
☞ Chill and shape truffles as above. Roll in sugar or chocolate strands.

Cherry Chocolate Crunch

INGREDIENTS

SERVES 8-10

¹/₂ cup/100 g/4 oz plain (dark) chocolate in small pieces

¹/₂ cup/100 g/4 oz butter

1 egg

1 cup/100 g/4 oz digestive biscuits
(Graham crackers) crumbs

¹/₄ cup/50 g/2 oz glacé (candied) cherries, chopped

¹/₄ cup/50 ml/2 fl oz rum

2 tbsp/30 g chopped nuts

PREPARATION

☛ Melt the chocolate with the butter in the top of a double boiler.

☛ Lightly beat the egg and stir into the melted chocolate.

☛ Combine all the ingredients and mix well so that the biscuit crumbs are well coated with chocolate.

☛ Turn the chocolate mixture into a well greased 20 cm/8 in cake pan.

☛ Chill for at least 8 hours before serving.

Choc Nut Slice

INGREDIENTS

SERVES 8—10

¾ cup/175 g/6 oz plain (dark) chocolate in small pieces

¾ cup/100 g/4 oz icing (confectioners') sugar

½ cup/100 g/4 oz peanut butter

1 tbsp/15 g butter

a pinch of salt

2 tsp/10 g instant coffee granules

¼ cup/50 ml/2 fl oz boiling water

1 egg

1 tsp/5 ml vanilla essence (extract)

2½ cups/300 g/10 oz biscuit (cookie) crumbs

PREPARATION

☛ Melt the chocolate in the top of a double boiler.
☛ Sift the icing sugar.
☛ Mix together the melted chocolate, sugar, peanut butter, butter and salt.
☛ Dissolve the instant coffee granules in boiling water.
☛ Lightly beat the egg.
☛ Add the coffee, egg, vanilla and crumbs to the chocolate. Mix well so that the crumbs are well coated.
☛ Line a loaf pan with foil.
☛ Spoon the chocolate mixture in the loaf pan. Smooth the surface and cover with foil. Freeze for at least 4 hours.
☛ Remove from the freezer one hour before you are ready to serve. Slice and arrange on serving dishes.

TO SERVE

Decorate with whipped cream.

Red Velvet Cake

INGREDIENTS

SERVES 10–12

½ cup/100 g/4 oz margarine	1 tsp/5 ml vanilla essence (extract)
1½ cups/350 g/12 oz sugar	1 tsp/5 g bicarbonate of soda (baking soda)
2 eggs	1 tsp/5 ml white wine vinegar
¼ cup/50 ml/2 fl oz red food colouring	oven temperature 180°C/350°F/Gas 4
2 tbsp/30 g unsweetened cocoa	**ICING**
2¼ cups/250 g/9 oz plain (all-purpose) flour	3 tbsp/45 ml flour
1 tsp/5 g salt	1 cup/225 g/8 oz sugar
1 cup/225 ml/8 fl oz buttermilk	1 cup/225 ml/8 fl oz milk
	1 cup/225 g/8 oz butter
	1 tsp/5 ml vanilla essence (extract)

PREPARATION

☛ Cream the margarine and sugar until fluffy.

☛ Beat in the eggs.

☛ Make a paste of the food colouring and cocoa. Add to the butter mixture and blend well.

☛ Sift the flour and salt. Gradually add to the butter mixture, alternating with the buttermilk and vanilla.

☛ Stir the bicarbonate of soda into the vinegar in a large spoon, holding it over the mixing bowl as it foams. Add to the cake mixture stirring well.

☛ Grease two 20 cm/8 in cake pans. Divide the mixture between the two pans and bake for 30 minutes. Cool.

☛ To prepare the icing, stir the flour, sugar and milk over a very low heat until thick.

☛ Cream the butter with the vanilla until it is very light.

☛ Beat the cooked mixture into the butter until the icing has the texture of whipped cream.

☛ To assemble the cake, place one layer, upside down, on a serving dish. Spread with one third of the icing. Gently place the second layer, right side up, on top. Spread the sides of the cake with icing and do the top last.

Chocolate Chip Cake

INGREDIENTS

SERVES 8–12

½ cup/100 g/4 oz margarine

⅓ cup/75 g/3 oz soft brown sugar

¾ cup/100 g/4 oz ground hazelnuts (filberts)

¾ cup/75 g/3 oz plain (all-purpose) flour

1 tsp/5 g baking powder

3 eggs, separated

1 orange

¼ cup/50 g/2 oz chocolate pieces

oven temperature 170°C/325°F/Gas 3

PREPARATION

☛ Cream the margarine and sugar until they are light and fluffy.

☛ Add the nuts, flour, baking powder, egg yolks and the grated rind and juice of the orange. Mix well.

☛ Fold in the chocolate pieces.

☛ Whisk the egg whites until they are stiff but not dry. Gently fold into the cake mixture starting with just one spoonful and gradually adding the remainder.

☛ Grease an 18 cm/7 in square cake pan and line with greaseproof (waxed) paper.

☛ Turn the mixture into the pan and bake for 45 minutes.

☛ For a larger cake double all the ingredients and use a roasting pan, 23 × 28 cm/9 × 11 in.

Chocolate Rum Cake

INGREDIENTS

SERVES 6

1 tbsp/15 ml water

2 tbsp/25 g/1 oz sugar

½ cup/100 g/4 oz plain (dark) chocolate in small pieces

1 tbsp/15 ml rum, brandy or Grand Marnier

1¼ cups/300 ml/½ pt double (heavy) cream

20 sponge fingers (Boudoir biscuits)

½ cup/100 ml/4 fl oz cold black coffee

2 tbsp/25 g grated chocolate

PREPARATION

☛ Heat the water and sugar, stirring constantly, until the sugar has dissolved. Leave to cool.

☛ Melt the chocolate in the top of a double boiler.

☛ Add the cooled syrup, stirring constantly.

☛ Stir in the rum, brandy or Grand Marnier and 3 tbsp/45 ml cream.

☛ Arrange half of the sponge fingers in the bottom of a serving dish.

☛ Carefully sprinkle the coffee over the sponge fingers, enough to just moisten them.

☛ Spread half of the chocolate mixture over the top.

☛ Arrange a second layer of sponge fingers gently over the chocolate.

☛ Sprinkle with coffee and spread with chocolate as before.

☛ Whisk the remaining cream until it is just firm. Spread over the top of the cake (and the sides if you are using a flat plate), and chill for 1 hour.

TO SERVE

Decorate with grated chocolate.

Brownies

INGREDIENTS

SERVES 8–12

5 tbsp/65 g/2½ oz margarine

2 eggs

1 cup/225 g/8 oz sugar

¾ cup/75 g/3 oz plain (all-purpose) flour

1 tsp/5 g baking powder

3 tbsp/45 g unsweetened cocoa

1 cup/100 g/4 oz walnuts, chopped

oven temperature 180°C/375°F/Gas 4

PREPARATION

☞ Melt the margarine and leave to cool slightly.
☞ Beat the eggs and sugar until they are very light and fluffy.
☞ Sift together the flour and baking powder.
☞ Stir the flour, baking powder, cocoa, walnuts and melted margarine into the egg mixture. Mix well.
☞ Grease a 20 cm/8 in square baking pan.
☞ Spoon the brownie mixture into the pan and bake for 30 minutes.
☞ Cut the brownies while they are warm, but leave in the pan until they have cooled completely.

Florentines

INGREDIENTS

MAKES 40

½ cup/100 g/4 oz butter

½ cup/100 g/4 oz sugar

1 tbsp/15 ml double (heavy) cream

1 cup/100 g/4 oz almonds, chopped

¼ cup/50 g/2 oz glacé (candied) cherries

⅓ cup/50 g/2 oz sultanas (white raisins)

oven temperature 180°C/350°F/Gas 4

ICING

1⅔ cups/225 g/8 oz icing (confectioners') sugar

6 tbsp/90 g unsweetened cocoa

¼ cup/50 g/2 oz butter

6 tbsp/90 ml milk

1 tsp/5 ml vanilla essence (extract)

PREPARATION

☛ Place the butter, sugar and cream in a heavy-bottomed pan. Heat over a low flame, stirring constantly, until the sugar has dissolved.

☛ Remove the butter from the heat and stir in the chopped nuts and fruit.

☛ Grease flat baking trays and line with rice paper or edible parchment.

☛ Drop small spoonfuls of the cookie mixture onto the baking trays. Be sure to leave as much space as possible between them as they spread while they are baking.

☛ Bake for 10 minutes and leave to cool on the trays for at least 5 minutes.

☛ Move to a cooling rack and trim extra paper.

☛ To make the icing, sift together the sugar and cocoa.

☛ Combine half of the sugar with the butter and beat well.

☛ Gradually add the remaining sugar, alternating with the combined milk and vanilla.

☛ When the Florentines have cooled completely, turn them upside down and spread with the icing. Leave to set before serving.

Chocolate Fondue

INGREDIENTS

SERVES 6

1¼ cups/300 g/10 oz sugar

⅔ cup/150 ml/¼ pt water

½ cup/100 g/4 oz plain (dark) chocolate in small pieces

½ cup/100 g/4 oz milk (light) chocolate in small pieces

5 tbsp/75 g/2½ oz butter

2½ tbsp/40 ml double (heavy) cream

5 tbsp/75 ml rum, brandy or Grand Marnier

PREPARATION

☛ Heat the sugar and water over a low heat, stirring constantly, until the sugar has dissolved. Leave to cool.

☛ Melt the chocolate with the butter and cream in the top of a double boiler. Stir occasionally.

☛ Remove the melted chocolate from the heat. Gradually stir in the sweetened water and mix well.

☛ Stir in the rum, brandy or Grand Marnier.

Chocolate Orange Mousse

INGREDIENTS

SERVES 4—6

½ cup/100 g/4 oz plain (dark) chocolate in small pieces

4 eggs, separated

¼ cup/50 ml/2 fl oz Grand Marnier or Cointreau

¼ cup/50 ml/2 fl oz orange juice

½ cup/100 ml/4 fl oz double (heavy) cream

PREPARATION

☛ Melt the chocolate in the top of a double boiler.
☛ Beat the egg yolks with the melted chocolate until smooth.
☛ Stir in the liqueur and orange juice.
☛ Lightly whip the cream and fold into the chocolate mixture.
☛ Whisk the egg whites until they are stiff but not dry. Gently fold into the mousse, starting with just one spoonful and gradually adding the remainder.
☛ Spoon the mousse into small dishes.
☛ Chill for at least 2 hours before serving.

VARIATION

For a Coffee Chocolate Mousse, substitute Tia Maria or Drambuie for the Grand Marnier and strong black coffee for the orange juice.

Diced pieces of mint sweets (candy) or fresh fruit can be stirred into the mousse before chilling.

This mousse can also be used as a filling for Ice Cream Bombe (see page 91).

Chestnut Mousse

INGREDIENTS

SERVES 4–6

6 tbsp/90 g butter

1 cup/225 g/8 oz unsweetened chestnut purée

2 eggs, separated

2 tbsp/30 g sugar

1½ tbsp/25 g unsweetened cocoa

1½ tbsp/25 g ground almonds

1½ tbsp/25 ml brandy

½ cup/100 ml/4 fl oz double (heavy) cream

8–10 blanched almonds

1 tbsp/15 g chocolate strands

PREPARATION

☛ Melt the butter. Leave to cool.
☛ Beat the chestnut purée until it is smooth.
☛ Add the butter, egg yolks, sugar, cocoa, almonds and brandy. Mix well. Whisk the egg whites until they are stiff but not dry. Gently fold into the chestnut mixture, starting with one spoonful and gradually adding the remainder.

TO SERVE

Turn the mousse into dishes. Decorate with lightly whipped cream, almonds and chocolate strands.
Chill for at least 2 hours before serving.

VARIATION

¼ cup/50 g/2 oz butter

¼ cup/50 g/2 oz sugar

½ cup/100 g/4 oz plain (dark) chocolate in small pieces

1 cup/225 g/8 oz unsweetened chestnut purée

¼ tsp/1¼ ml vanilla essence (extract)

½ cup/100 ml/4 fl oz double (heavy) cream, whipped

8–10 blanched almonds

1 tbsp/15 g chocolate strands

PREPARATION

☛ Cream the butter and sugar until they are light and fluffy.
☛ Melt the chocolate in the top of a double boiler.
☛ Combine the chocolate, butter mixture, chestnut purée and vanilla. Beat until smooth.
☛ Grease a small loaf pan and line with greaseproof (waxed) paper. Spoon the mousse into the pan, smooth the surface and chill for at least 8 hours.

TO SERVE

Turn out onto a serving dish. Decorate with cream, nuts and chocolate.

Chocolate Crispies

MAKES 24

¾ cup/175 g/6 oz butter

¾ cup/175 g/6 oz chocolate

¾ cup/175 ml/6 fl oz golden (light corn) syrup

3 cups/175 g/6 oz cornflakes or rice crispies

PREPARATION

☛ Melt the butter, chocolate and syrup together in the top of a double boiler. Mix well.

☛ Pour the sauce over the cornflakes or rice crispies and stir well.

☛ Place 24 paper cups (as for muffins or cupcakes) in a pan and spoon the cereal mixture into the cases.

☛ Leave to set for at least 8 hours.

VARIATION

Press the cereal mixture into the paper cups leaving a hollow space in the centre which can later be filled with fruit and/or cream.

Ice Cream

BOMBE   91

EASY ICE CREAM   92

BUTTERSCOTCH SAUCE   93

CHOCOLATE FUDGE SAUCE   94

QUICK FRUIT SAUCE   94

SUMMER SAUCE   95

BLACK CHERRY SAUCE   95

MARSHMALLOW CRUNCH   96

ICE CREAM CAKE   99

FRUIT SURPRISE   100

TORTONI   101

SAILORS' DELIGHT   103

DUTCH APPLE SPECIAL   104

SUNDAE SUPREME   105

Opposite: Four seasons sorbet

Introduction

ICE CREAM as a dessert is both light and refreshing. If you feel inspired to make your own ice cream, the flavours can be unlimited. But the selection of commercial ice creams and sorbets (sherbets) is now so wide and of such a high quality that virtually everyone can find something to suit in the freezer cabinet.

Making or selecting the ice cream, however, is only the first step to serving it as a dessert. Nothing looks more attractive than a dish piled high with scoops of different coloured and flavoured ices. A few mint leaves arranged between the scoops offers an elegant, but very simple, finale for the most special dinner party. On the other hand, it is easy to have your own "ice cream parlour" at home, with an assortment of biscuits (cookies) or wafers, sauces, nuts, fruit and, of course, a huge dish of whipped cream. There are any number of delicious concoctions you can make. Ice cream can be sandwiched between two giant cookies and frozen until it is firm. Profiteroles (eclairs) can be filled with ice cream and topped with chocolate sauce. Bombes combine ice cream and sorbets (sherbets) with mousses or fruit for contrast in both flavour and appearance. None are as difficult to make as you might think!

Ice cream is by no means for children only as some people think. The Victorians were renowned for their long and very heavy meals and midway through these banquets they regularly took a pause to refresh their palates with sorbets (sherbets) and ices. One of the earliest desserts recorded was snow sweetened with honey, and eaten by the Romans. No wonder the Italians produce some of the world's best ice cream – they had a head start! Crushed ice with fruit syrups have been popular for as long as anyone can remember. Ice cream and sorbet indulgence, then, is a precedent which has been well set, for us all to enjoy.

Bombe

INGREDIENTS

SERVES 8

2½ cups/550 g/1 pt ice cream

1¼ cups/275 ml/½ pt sorbet (sherbet)

½ cup/100 ml/4 fl oz double (heavy) cream

Pieces of crystallized fruit

PREPARATION

☞ Remove half of the ice cream from the freezer and leave until slightly softened. Press over the base and up the sides of a medium sized mould (mold) or pudding bowl. Cover and return to the freezer until firm.
☞ Remove the sorbet from the freezer and leave until slightly softened. Press into the middle of the mould, cover and return to the freezer.
☞ Remove the remaining ice cream, which should be a different flavour, and leave to soften. Spread over the surface of the sorbet, cover and refreeze.

TO SERVE

Run a warm cloth over the surface of the mould, invert and turn out onto an attractive dish. Smooth with a knife. Decorate with piped, whipped cream and pieces of crystallized fruit.

VARIATIONS

Beat into slightly softened vanilla ice cream an assortment of dried fruit which has been soaked in rum or sherry and some chopped crystallized fruit. Fill the mould and freeze until firm.
Soak fresh or dried fruit in liqueur and pour into the bombe before adding the sorbet (sherbet).
Replace the sorbet with a chocolate or chestnut mousse.

Easy Ice Cream

INGREDIENTS

SERVES 8
4 eggs, separated
½ tsp/2½ ml vanilla essence (extract)
¾ cup/100 g/4 oz icing (confectioners') sugar
1¼ cups/300 ml/½ pt double (heavy) cream

PREPARATION

☞ Beat the egg yolks with the vanilla and sifted sugar until the mixture is very thick and almost white.

☞ Lightly whip the cream until it is just beginning to thicken. Gently fold into the yolks.

☞ Whisk the egg whites until they are stiff but not dry. Gently fold one spoonful into the ice cream mixture. Gradually add the remaining egg whites.

☞ If you are adding flavouring, blend in carefully at this stage.

☞ Turn the cream into a large freezer tray or plastic box and cover. Stir occasionally during freezing.

Butterscotch Sauce

INGREDIENTS

SERVES 4

¼ cup/50 g/2 oz butter

¼ cup/50 g/2 oz light brown sugar

2 tbsp/30 ml golden (light corn) syrup

PREPARATION

☛ Combine all ingredients in a heavy-bottomed pan. Heat over a low flame, stirring constantly, until the sugar dissolves and the sauce comes to the boil. Serve hot or cold.

Chocolate Fudge Sauce

Quick Fruit Sauce

INGREDIENTS

SERVES 8—10

1 cup/100 g/4 oz unsweetened cocoa

¾ cup/175 g/6 oz sugar

½ tsp/2½ ml salt

1 tbsp/15 g cornflour (cornstarch)

½ cup/100 ml/4 fl oz golden (light corn) syrup

½ cup/100 ml/4 fl oz milk

2 tsp/10 ml vanilla essence (extract)

2 tbsp/30 g butter

PREPARATION

☛ Combine all ingredients in a heavy-bottomed pan. Heat over a low flame, stirring constantly, until well blended and the sauce comes to the boil. Serve hot or cold.

INGREDIENTS

SERVES 6

2 cups/450 g/1 lb fruit

icing (confectioners') sugar

PREPARATION

☛ Stone, liquidize and strain any soft fruit in season eg peaches, berries, mango etc. Sweeten to taste and spoon over ice cream.

Summer Sauce

Black Cherry Sauce

INGREDIENTS

SERVES 8—10

2 cups/225 g/8 oz redcurrants

2 cups/225 g/8 oz blackcurrants

1³/4 cups/225 g/8 oz raspberries

¹/2 cup/100 g/4 oz sugar

2 tbsp/30 ml orange juice

2 tsp/10 g cornflour (cornstarch)

2 tbsp/30 ml water

PREPARATION

☛ Place the fruit, sugar and orange juice in a heavy-bottomed pan on a low heat. Cook gently until the fruit is soft.
☛ Combine the cornflour and water. Stir into the cooked fruit and bring to the boil, stirring constantly. Heat until the sauce has thickened.

INGREDIENTS

SERVES 8—10

3 cups/450 g/1 lb black cherries

¹/4 cup/50 g/2 oz sugar

¹/4 cup/50 ml/2 fl oz water

1 tsp/5 g cornflour (cornstarch)

1 tbsp/15 ml water

PREPARATION

☛ Place the fruit, sugar and water in a heavy-bottomed pan on a very low heat. Cook gently until the fruit is soft.
☛ Combine the cornflour and water. Stir into the cooked fruit and bring to the boil, stirring constantly. Heat until the sauce has thickened.
☛ If you are serving black cherry sauce for a special occasion, stir in a few spoonfuls of kirsch.

Marshmallow Crunch

INGREDIENTS

SERVES 4

8 small meringues

2½ cups/550 ml/1 pt ice cream

8 small marshmallows

2 cups/450 ml/16 oz chocolate or fruit sauce

PREPARATION

☞ Crush the meringues coarsely and arrange at the bottom of each serving dish. Top with two scoops of ice cream. Add the marshmallows and spoon over the sauce.

☞ As an alternative, the meringues can be left whole and sandwiched together with the ice cream. The marshmallows and sauce are arranged on top. If you like your sundaes gooey, melt the marshmallows!

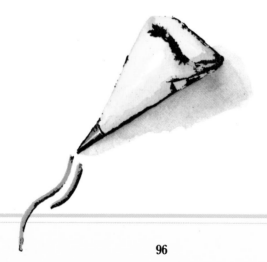

Divine
Desserts
ICE CREAM

Ice Cream Cake

INGREDIENTS

SERVES 6—8
3 eggs
½ cup/100 g/4 oz sugar
1 cup + 2 tbsp/100 g/4 oz plain (all-purpose) flour
1 tbsp/15 ml hot water
1 cup/225 g/8 oz ice cream
oven temperature 220°C/425°F/Gas 7

PREPARATION

☛ Whisk the eggs and sugar until they are very light and creamy. Gradually fold in the sifted flour. Very gently stir in the water.

☛ Grease a 33 × 23 cm/13 × 9 in Swiss (jelly) roll tin and line with greaseproof (waxed) paper. Carefully spread the cake mixture over the pan. Bake for 7–9 minutes or until firm to the touch.

☛ Invert the cake onto a clean sheet of paper and roll loosely. Leave to cool.

☛ Remove the ice cream from the freezer and leave to soften slightly.

☛ When the cake has cooled, unroll it, and spread with ice cream. Roll the cake and freeze until the ice cream is firm.

☛ Remove the cake from the freezer 15 minutes before serving.

TO SERVE

Accompany with your favourite sauce or a bowl of whipped cream.

VARIATIONS

For a chocolate ice cream cake, substitute 1 tbsp/15 g unsweetened cocoa for the same amount of flour.

Before freezing the ice cream cake, the surface may be decorated with either whipped cream or butter cream icing.

Substitute sliced pound cake or Madeira cake for the Swiss (jelly) roll.

Slice the top layer off a ring-shaped cake, hollow out the base and fill with ice cream and fruit. Replace the lid. Freeze and decorate as above.

Fruit Surprise

INGREDIENTS

SERVES 8

8 oranges or lemons, or 1 pineapple

2½ cups/550 g/1 pt ice cream or sorbet

PREPARATION

☛ Remove the ice cream or sorbet (sherbet) from the freezer and leave to slightly soften for approximately 30 minutes. Use a flavour you think will go well with the fruit you have chosen.

☛ Cut the top off the orange or lemon, or cut the pineapple in half. Carefully remove the fruit from its shell, leaving enough to keep the shape of the fruit. Chop coarsely and mix into the softened ice cream or sorbet (sherbet).

☛ Spoon the mixture back into the fruit shell and return to the freezer. Remove 15 minutes before serving.

VARIATION

After removing the fruit from its shell, mix with alcohol of virtually any sort – brandy, gin, liqueur – and leave to soak for 1 hour. Put the fruit back in its shell and top with the ice cream or sorbet (sherbet).

Freeze until firm.

Tortoni

INGREDIENTS

SERVES 8

5 eggs, separated

⅓ cup/75 g/3 oz sugar

2½ cups/550 ml/1 pt double (heavy) cream

1½ cups/175 g/6 oz macaroon or ratafia crumbs

⅓ cup/75 ml/3 fl oz Marsala or sweet sherry

PREPARATION

☛ Beat the egg yolks with the sugar until thick and almost white.

☛ Whisk the cream until it is just starting to thicken. Stir into the eggs. Stir in ¾ of the crumbs and the wine.

☛ Whisk the egg whites until they are stiff but not dry. Gently fold one spoonful into the cream mixture then gradually add the remainder.

☛ Pour the cream into a soufflé dish or individual ramekins (serving dishes) and freeze, stirring occasionally. Remove 15 minutes before serving. Gently pan the remaining crumbs over the surface and press onto the top.

Sailors' Delight

SERVES 4

1⅓ cups/225 ml/8 oz mincemeat

¼ cup/50 ml/2 fl oz rum

2½ cups/550 g/1 pt ice cream

PREPARATION

☞ Gently heat the mincemeat with the rum. Spoon over the ice cream.

Dutch Apple Special

INGREDIENTS

SERVES 4

2²/₃ cups/450 g/1 lb apples, cored and sliced

2 tbsp/30 ml water

¹/₄ cup/50 g/2 oz brown sugar

¹/₃ cup/50 g/2 oz raisins

1 tsp/5 g cinnamon

¹/₂ tsp/2¹/₂ g nutmeg

2¹/₂ cups/550 g/1 pt ice cream

PREPARATION

☛ Place apples in a pan with the water. Cook over a low heat until the apples are soft.

☛ Purée the apples and stir in the sugar until it has melted. Add the raisins, cinnamon and nutmeg.

TO SERVE

Arrange two scoops of ice cream in each serving dish. Spoon the warm apple sauce over the top and serve immediately.

Sundae Supreme

INGREDIENTS

SERVES 4

2½ cups/550 g/1 pt ice cream

8 wafers or cookies

2 cups/450 ml/16 oz chocolate or fruit sauce

1 cup/225 ml/8 oz whipped cream

⅓ cup/50 g/2 oz toasted nuts, chopped

4 glacé (candied) or maraschino cherries

PREPARATION

☛ Arrange two scoops of ice cream in each serving dish, preferably two flavours.

☛ Crumble the wafers or cookies and sprinkle over the ice cream. Pour on the sauce. Top with whipped cream, piled as high as you can, and scatter chopped nuts on top. Crown each sundae with a cherry.

Soufflés

CLASSIC SOUFFLE   109

CHOCOLATE SOUFFLE   110

ORANGE SOUFFLE   111

RED FRUIT SOUFFLE   113

CHILLED ORANGE SOUFFLE   114

HOT FRUIT SOUFFLE   115

Opposite: Classic soufflé (see page 109)

Divine
Desserts
SOUFFLES

Introduction

NYONE WHO HAS EVER made a successful soufflé will tell you that it is the perfect way to impress dinner guests. The thought of attempting a soufflé can strike terror into the heart of the novice cook but, once the technique has been mastered, it is by no means a difficult dessert to produce.

Although the flavourings used for a soufflé can be left to the imagination, there are certain iron clad rules which must be acknowledged. Firstly, the egg whites must be whisked to incorporate as much air as possible. Air is the very essence of a soufflé, causing it to rise and remain light. Secondly, do not let the whisked egg whites stand for more than a few minutes before folding them into the other ingredients. Up to this stage the mixture can be prepared in advance, but if the whites are not used immediately, the air subsides. Because soufflés cook quickly, the oven must be preheated. To test that the soufflé is properly cooked, a knife or skewer can be inserted into the middle. If it comes out slightly moist, the soufflé is as the French like it. If it comes out dry, it is as the British like it. In either case it should be well risen and crisp on top.

This chapter includes recipes for chilled soufflés which are both smooth and airy. They do not need to be cooked and use cream, egg whites and sometimes gelatine (gelatin) to set them while they chill. As they do not rise, a collar is tied around the top of the soufflé dish so that it can be filled beyond its depth and then removed after it has set to give an impression of height.

Hot soufflés must be served immediately after cooking. Once the air trapped in the soufflé hits the cooler air of the kitchen, it begins to fall. So even if your dessert course must be delayed while the soufflé cooks, do not, under any circumstances, make the dessert wait while you finish your conversation! Cooking time can be cut to a minimum by using individual ramekins (serving dishes). In that way you can slip out to the kitchen, whisk the egg whites and bake the soufflé while the table is being cleared for dessert. Once you are committed to a soufflé you must remember that timing is crucial but if you stick to the rules, the result should be perfect every time.

Classic Soufflé

INGREDIENTS

SERVES 4—6
¼ cup/25 g/1 oz plain (all-purpose) flour
⅔ cup/150 ml/¼ pt milk
3 tbsp/45 g sugar
a pinch of salt
2 egg yolks
1 tbsp/15 g butter
3 egg whites

oven temperature 220°C/425°F/Gas 7

PREPARATION

☛ Mix the flour with enough milk to make a paste.

☛ Heat the remaining milk with the sugar and salt. When the milk has reached boiling point, stir in the flour paste and the flavouring of your choice (see below). Continue to cook for 2–3 minutes.

☛ Remove the sauce from the heat.

☛ Stir in the egg yolks and butter until well blended and the butter has melted.

☛ Whisk the egg whites until they are stiff but not dry. Gently fold into the sauce, starting with just one spoonful and gradually adding the remainder.

☛ Turn into a greased 1 l/2 pt soufflé dish and sprinkle with sugar. Bake for 10–12 minutes or until well risen. Sprinkle with sugar approximately 2 minutes before the cooking is complete in order to glaze the soufflé.

VARIATION INGREDIENTS

SERVES 4—6
¼ cup/25 g/1 oz plain (all-purpose) flour
3 tbsp/45 g sugar
a pinch of salt
6 tbsp/75 ml milk
3 eggs, separated
1 tbsp/15 g butter

PREPARATION

☛ Combine the flour, sugar and salt with the milk and flavouring of your choice (see below).

☛ Heat, stirring continuously, until it reaches boiling point.

☛ Remove from the heat and stir in the egg yolks and butter. Mix until the sauce is well blended and the butter has melted.

☛ Fold in the stiffly beaten egg whites and complete as above.

FLAVOURINGS

☛ Stir 2 tbsp/30 g diced stem ginger and a large pinch of powdered ginger into the sauce before adding the egg whites.

☛ Stir 2 tbsp/30 ml liqueur into the sauce before adding the egg whites.

☛ Add 2 tbsp/30 g soaked or poached prunes, apricots or figs to the sauce. The fruit may be either diced or puréed.

☛ Add 2 tbsp/30 g plain or roasted almonds, hazelnuts (filberts), walnuts or chopped peanut brittle. The nuts may be chopped or ground. Stir into the sauce before adding the egg whites.

☛ Stone 1 cup/100 g/4 oz cherries, sprinkle with sugar and cook on a low flame until the fruit is soft. Chop or purée the cherries and stir into the sauce before adding the egg whites.

☛ Thinly peel a lemon, lime or orange, taking care to remove all the pith. Cut into strips and heat with the milk when preparing the sauce.

☛ Stir 2 tbsp/30 g chopped praline, peanut brittle or rock (peppermint stick) into the sauce before adding the egg whites.

Chocolate Soufflé

INGREDIENTS

SERVES 4

2 tbsp/30 g butter

2 tbsp/30 g plain (all-purpose) flour

¾ cup/175 ml/6 fl oz milk

½ tsp/2½ ml vanilla essence (extract)

⅓ cup/40 g/1½ oz plain (dark) chocolate, chopped
or grated

3 eggs, separated

¼ cup/50 g/2 oz sugar

oven temperature 180°C/350°F/Gas 4

PREPARATION

☛ Melt the butter in a heavy-bottomed pan.
☛ Mix in the flour and continue to cook, stirring continuously, until the butter absorbs the flour.
☛ Gradually add the milk, vanilla and chocolate. Continue to cook, stirring constantly, until the chocolate has melted and the sauce has thickened.

☛ Whisk the egg yolks with the sugar until they are light and frothy.
☛ Pour the egg yolk mixture into the chocolate sauce and stir thoroughly but gently.
☛ Whisk the egg whites until they are stiff but not dry. Gently fold into the chocolate mixture, starting with just one spoonful and gradually adding the remainder.
☛ Grease a 1 litre/2 pint soufflé dish and sprinkle the base with sugar.
☛ Pour the mixture into the prepared dish. Make a deep cut around the mixture, approximately 2½ cm/1 in from the edge.
☛ Bake the soufflé until it is well risen and set. Sprinkle with sifted icing (confectioners') sugar and serve immediately.

VARIATIONS

For a Caramel Soufflé, omit the chocolate and heat 3 tbsp/45 g sugar in a heavy-bottomed pan until the sugar has melted and browned. Stir into the thickened sauce before adding the egg yolk mixture.
For a Vanilla Soufflé, heat the milk with a vanilla pod and leave to stand for 1 hour. Remove the vanilla pod and use the milk to make the sauce as described above.

Orange Soufflé

INGREDIENTS

SERVES 4

4 large oranges

1 lemon

2 tbsp/30 g butter

2 tbsp/30 g plain (all-purpose) flour

4 eggs, separated

3 tbsp/45 g sugar

oven temperature 200°C/400°F/Gas 6

PREPARATION

☛ Cut the oranges in half crossways and carefully remove the flesh. Squeeze to extract the juice.
☛ Add the juice of the lemon to the juice of the oranges.
☛ Carefully cut strips of peel off half of each orange. Blanch in boiling water for 5 minutes.
☛ Melt the butter in a heavy-bottomed pan. Add the flour and cook, stirring constantly, until all the butter has been absorbed.

☛ Slowly stir in the fruit juice and peel, stirring constantly, and cook until the sauce thickens and comes to the boil. Simmer gently for 2 minutes.
☛ Whisk the egg yolks with the sugar until they are thick and frothy. Stir into the sauce.
☛ Whisk the egg whites until they are stiff but not dry. Gently fold into the sauce, starting with just one spoonful and gradually adding the remainder.
☛ Grease a 575 ml/1 pt soufflé dish and sprinkle the base with sugar. Pour in the soufflé mixture and bake for approximately 25 minutes or until well risen. Sprinkle with icing (confectioners') sugar before serving.

VARIATIONS

Bake the soufflé in the orange shells allowing 20 minutes to cook.
Stir 1 tbsp/15 ml of Cointreau or Grand Marnier into the soufflé mixture before adding the egg whites.
To glaze the soufflé, sprinkle icing (confectioners') sugar on 2–3 minutes before it has finished cooking.

Red Fruit Soufflé

INGREDIENTS

SERVES 4

1½–2 cups/225 g/8 oz raspberries, strawberries, red or black currants
½ cup/100 g/4 oz sugar
1 tbsp/15 ml kirsch, cassis or frambois
2 tbsp/30 g cornflour (cornstarch)
1¼ cups/300 ml/½ pt milk
2 eggs
¾ cup/175 ml/6 fl oz double (heavy) cream

PREPARATION

☛ If using raspberries or strawberries, sieve or purée the fruit and mix with the sugar. If using red or black currants, sprinkle with sugar and heat in a heavy-bottomed pan until the berries are soft. Cool slightly and sieve or purée.

☛ Stir in the liqueur.

☛ Mix the cornflour with enough milk to make a smooth paste. Heat the remaining milk until it just reaches boiling point. Pour over the cornflour and mix well.

☛ Lightly beat the eggs and stir into the hot milk.

☛ Return to the heat and cook, stirring constantly, until it begins to thicken. Leave to cool.

☛ Combine the fruit purée with the sauce.

☛ Whisk the cream until it is just thick enough to hold its shape. Gently fold into the fruit sauce.

☛ Tie a paper collar around the outside of a 575 ml/ 1 pt soufflé dish so that it extends 5 cm/2 in above the top of the dish. Pour the soufflé mixture into the dish and chill overnight or until firm.

TO SERVE

Garnish the soufflé with fresh fruit.

Chilled Orange Soufflé

INGREDIENTS

SERVES 4
2 eggs
½ cup/100 g/4 oz sugar
⅔ cup/150 ml/¼ pt double (heavy) cream
1 orange
1 tbsp/15 ml Cointreau or Grand Marnier

PREPARATION

☛ Whisk one of the eggs and the yolk from the second with the sugar until very light and frothy.

☛ Whisk the cream until it is just firm enough to hold its shape. Stir in the finely grated rind of the orange, 2 tbsp/30 ml of its juice and the liqueur.

☛ Combine the yolk and cream mixtures.

☛ Whisk the remaining egg white until it is stiff but not dry. Gently fold into the soufflé, starting with just one spoonful and gradually adding the remainder. Spoon into individual soufflé dishes and chill overnight or until set.

Hot Fruit Soufflé

INGREDIENTS

SERVES 4

approx 1 cup/225 g/8 oz soft fruit

½ cup/100 g/4 oz sugar

1 tbsp/15 ml liqueur

5 egg whites

oven temperature 180°C/350°F/Gas 4

PREPARATION

☛ Sieve or purée the fruit with the sugar.

☛ Stir in the liqueur.

☛ Whisk the egg whites until they are stiff but not dry. Fold into the fruit purée, starting with just one spoonful and gradually adding the remainder.

☛ Turn the soufflé into a greased 1½ l/2½ pt dish which has been sprinkled with sugar. Bake for 30 minutes or until well risen.

TO SERVE

Sprinkle with icing (confectioners') sugar just before serving.

VARIATION

Substitute chestnut purée for the fruit. Beat the yolks into the sweetened purée and then fold in the stiffly beaten whites. Bake as described above.

Puddings

BAKED SEMOLINA PUDDING 119

SUSSEX POND PUDDING 120

UPSIDE DOWN LEMON PUDDING 121

QUEEN OF PUDDINGS 122

CHOCOLATE SEMOLINA PUDDING 123

BREAD PUDDING 124

RICE PUDDING 125

STEAMED FRUIT PUDDING 126

SUMMER PUDDING 127

Opposite: Baked semolina pudding (see page 119)

Introduction

THE WORD PUDDING evokes different desserts to all of us. Americans think of pudding as blancmange and other milk desserts of rice, macaroni or semolina. In Britain, childhood and school dinners come to mind with their baked rice and semolina puddings, steamed puddings filled with syrup or fruit, sponge rolls and custard. In fact, the word pudding in England is frequently used to mean a dessert of any kind.

Other Europeans and Asians don't always understand the meaning of pudding at all. Although desserts are frequently baked, boiled or steamed in the same manner as other well-known puddings, the word itself is unfamiliar. According to one definition, a pudding is a stuffing of fruit cooked in a casing of flour or a soft kind of cooked dish, usually farinaceous, commonly with milk, eggs and sugar etc. Spotted Dick and Jam Roly Poly fit into the first category – a dough or batter filled with currants and raisins – whereas a sponge spread with jam, then rolled and steamed falls into the second category. There are countless variations on farinaceous puddings throughout the world. There are versions of rice pudding, for instance, garnished with silver leaf in India, topped with meringue in Germany or puff pastry in Ireland and moulded with crystallized fruit in France.

The recipes in this chapter come primarily from England, where puddings have always been far more popular than any other country in the world. Puddings in England can be an art form – few other countries take such pride in their puddings. That is not to say that they cannot be cooked or appreciated in other countries. By using some of these traditional recipes comprising readily available ingredients, any kitchen in the world can create the aroma and warmth of these delightful nursery desserts.

Baked Semolina Pudding

INGREDIENTS

SERVES 4
1½ cups/350 ml/12 fl oz white wine
1¼ cups/300 ml/½ pt water
½ lemon
1 orange
a pinch of salt
⅔ cup/100 g/4 oz semolina (or farina)
½ cup/100 g/4 oz sugar
3 eggs, separated

PREPARATION

☛ Combine the wine, water, finely grated rinds of the lemon and orange, and the salt. Bring to the boil.

☛ Add the semolina to the pan, stirring constantly. Reduce the heat and simmer gently for approximately 5 minutes, or until the mixture is thick and smooth.

☛ Stir the sugar and the juice of the orange into the semolina.

☛ Continue to cook, stirring, until the pudding boils again.

☛ Remove the pan from the heat and stir in 2 egg yolks. Save the remaining yolk to use for another recipe.

☛ Whisk the egg whites until they are stiff but not dry. Fold gently into the semolina, starting with just one spoonful and gradually adding the remainder.

☛ Pour the pudding into one large or several small, wet moulds (molds). Chill before serving.

TO SERVE

Garnish with fresh or poached fruit or with a warm or cold fruit purée.

VARIATION

For a hot semolina pudding, place the mould (mold) in a roasting pan containing enough hot water to come halfway up the side of the dish. Cover the mould loosely with foil. Cook for 50–60 minutes at 170°C/325°F/Gas 3 or until the pudding has set. Serve from the dish or unmoulded.

Sussex Pond Pudding

INGREDIENTS

SERVES 8

3 cups/350 g/12 oz plain (all-purpose) flour

2 tsp/10 g baking powder

a pinch of salt

3/4 cup/175 g/6 oz suet or butter

3/4 cup/175 ml/6 fl oz milk or water

1 large lemon

1/2 cup/100 g/4 oz unsalted (sweet) butter

1/2 cup/100 g/4 oz brown or demerara sugar

PREPARATION

☛ Sift the flour with the baking powder and salt.

☛ Add the suet or butter and rub together until the mixture resembles coarse breadcrumbs.

☛ Bind the dough with milk or water.

☛ Knead lightly until the dough is smooth but not sticky. Cut into two pieces, one twice as large as the other.

☛ Roll the larger piece of dough until it is big enough to line the base and sides of a 1 1/2 pt pudding bowl. Gently press the dough into the basin.

☛ Cut the butter into small pieces and place half in the bottom of the lined basin. Sprinkle with half of the sugar.

☛ Prick the surface of the lemon all over with a fork so that the juice can flow when the pudding is cooked. Place on top of the bed of butter and sugar. Sprinkle with the remaining butter and sugar.

☛ Roll out the smaller piece of dough. Lay on top of the pudding and seal well.

☛ Cover the basin with a piece of greaseproof (waxed) paper and then a large piece of foil. Place in a pan containing enough boiling water to come halfway up the sides of the pudding basin. Steam for approximately 4 hours. Check the water occasionally and top up – it must not be allowed to boil away.

☛ Unmould (unmold) the pudding and serve immediately, either on its own or with custard.

Upside Down Lemon Pudding

INGREDIENTS

SERVES 6

6 tbsp/75 ml/3 oz butter or margarine

1/2 cup/100 g/4 oz sugar

3 lemons

3 eggs, separated

3/4 cup/75 g/3 oz flour

1 tsp/5 g baking powder

1 cup/225 ml/8 fl oz milk

oven temperature 180°C/350°F/Gas 4

PREPARATION

☛ Cream the butter or margarine with the sugar and finely grated lemon rind until very smooth.

☛ Beat the egg yolks into the sugar mixture.

☛ Sift the flour and baking powder. Fold into the sugar mixture, alternating with the milk and juice of the lemons.

☛ Whisk the egg whites until they are stiff but not dry. Carefully fold into the pudding batter, starting with one spoonful and gradually adding the remainder.

☛ Grease a deep pie dish, approximately 4 cups/ 900 ml/1½ pt. Pour the pudding into the dish and bake for 30 minutes or until it is golden. Serve warm or cold.

Queen of Puddings

INGREDIENTS

SERVES 4

2½ cups/550 ml/1 pt milk

¼ cup/50 g/2 oz butter

4 eggs, separated

1 lemon

½ cup/100 g/4 oz sugar

2 cups/100 g/4 oz fresh breadcrumbs

4 tbsp/60 g jam (preserves or jelly)

*oven temperature 180°C/350°F/Gas 4 and
150°C/300°F/Gas 2*

PREPARATION

☛ Heat the milk with the butter over a gentle heat until the butter has melted.

☛ Combine the egg yolks with the finely grated rind of the lemon and half of the sugar. Mix well.

☛ Pour the warm milk over the yolks and mix well.

☛ Stir in the breadcrumbs.

☛ Pour the pudding mixture (batter) into a well greased casserole or pie dish. Bake at the higher temperature for approximately 20 minutes, or until the custard has set.

☛ Heat the jam over a very low heat until it has melted. Spread carefully over the baked pudding.

☛ Whisk the egg whites until they are stiff but not dry. Gently fold in the remaining sugar. Spoon or pipe the meringue over the pudding. Be sure that all the edges are well sealed.

☛ Return the pudding to the oven and bake at the lower temperature for 10–20 minutes or until the meringue is brown and crisp.

Chocolate Semolina Pudding

INGREDIENTS

SERVES 4

2½ cups/550 ml/1 pt milk

2 tbsp/30 g butter

2 tbsp/30 g sugar

¼ cup/50 g/2 oz chocolate

4 tbsp/60 g semolina (or farina)

PREPARATION

☛ Heat the milk with the butter, sugar and chocolate until the chocolate has melted and the milk has reached boiling point.
☛ Sprinkle in the semolina and cook, stirring constantly, until the pudding thickens.
☛ Pour into one large or several small serving dishes and eat hot or cold.

VARIATIONS

For Butterscotch Pudding, use brown sugar instead of white, omit the chocolate and add 1 tbsp/15 ml golden (light corn) syrup.
For Holyrood Pudding, omit the chocolate and add 2 tsp/10 g orange marmalade. Stir in 1 tbsp/60 g ratafia or macaroon crumbs.
To make semolina puddings particularly light, cool slightly and fold in 2 beaten egg whites. The pudding should then be baked for 30 minutes at 150°C/300°F/Gas 2 or steamed for 1¼ hours.

Bread Pudding

INGREDIENTS

SERVES 8

1 small loaf white bread

1 cup/225 ml/8 fl oz milk

³/4 cup/175 g/6 oz sugar

½ cup/100 g/4 oz margarine

³/4 cup/175 ml/6 fl oz evaporated milk

2 tsp/10 ml vanilla essence (extract)

1 tsp/5 g mixed baking spice

1 tsp/5 g cinnamon or nutmeg

¹/3 cup/50 g/2 oz raisins

2 tbsp/30 g mixed peel

oven temperature 170°C/325°F/Gas 3

PREPARATION

☛ Remove the crust from the bread and cut the loaf into chunks. Pour over the milk, stir to make sure all the bread is moist, and leave to soak for 20 minutes.

☛ Cream the sugar and margarine until they are light and fluffy.

☛ Add the soaked bread, along with any milk remaining. Beat well.

☛ Stir in the evaporated milk, vanilla and spices.

☛ Fold in the raisins and mixed peel.

☛ Pour the pudding mixture into a well greased casserole dish and bake for 1 hour and 10 minutes or until firm to the touch and golden brown.

☛ Serve warm or cold.

Rice Pudding

INGREDIENTS

SERVES 8

⅔ cup/100 g/4 oz rice

1 cup/225 ml/8 fl oz water

a pinch of salt

½ cup/100 g/4 oz sugar

1 tsp/5 g cinnamon

3¾ cups/850 ml/1½ pt milk

2 eggs

⅓ cup/50 g/2 oz raisins

PREPARATION

☛ Wash the rice in running water until the water is clear. Place in a bowl with enough hot water to cover and leave to soak for 15 minutes.

☛ Drain the rice and place in a heavy-bottomed pan. Add the water and salt. Cover the pan, bring to the boil and then cook on a low heat until the water has been absorbed.

☛ Stir the sugar and half of the cinnamon into the cooked rice.

☛ Add the milk and mix well. Cook, uncovered, over a low heat until most of the milk has been absorbed. Stir occasionally.

☛ Lightly beat the eggs and mix into the rice. Continue to cook for 5 minutes.

☛ Stir in the raisins and turn the rice pudding into a serving dish. Combine the remaining cinnamon with a small spoonful of sugar and sprinkle over the pudding. Cool and chill before serving.

VARIATION

While the rice is cooking, soak the raisins in sherry or rum.

Serve the pudding as it is, or with single (light) cream and fresh raspberries for an extra treat.

For the simplest rice pudding of them all, combine 6 tbsp/90 g rice with 2 tbsp/30 g each of sugar and raisins. Pour in 5 cups/1.2 l/2 pt milk, sprinkle with cinnamon or nutmeg and bake in a very low oven until most of the milk has been absorbed.

Steamed Fruit Pudding

INGREDIENTS

SERVES 6
½ cup/50 g/2 oz plain (all-purpose) flour
1 tsp/5 g baking powder
3 cups/175 g/6 oz fresh breadcrumbs
½ cup/100 g/4 oz shredded suet
1 orange
½ tsp/2½ g mixed spice
a pinch of nutmeg
1 cup/175 g/6 oz dates
1 cup/175 g/6 oz figs
1 cup/175 g/6 oz raisins
2 eggs
2 tbsp/30 ml rum or brandy

PREPARATION

☛ Combine the sifted flour and baking powder with the breadcrumbs, suet and finely grated orange rind.

☛ Stir in the mixed spice, nutmeg, chopped dates, figs and raisins.

☛ Lightly beat the eggs with the juice of the orange and the rum or brandy. Add to the flour and fruit mixtures. Mix thoroughly so that the whole pudding is moist.

☛ Grease a 900 ml/1½ pt pudding bowl. Place a circle of greaseproof (waxed) paper in the base. Spoon the pudding into the bowl, but make sure that it is no more than ¾ full. Cover with a buttered circle of greaseproof paper, pleated in the middle – this allows the pudding room to rise during cooking. Cover the top of the bowl with a circle of pleated foil and tie securely.

☛ Place the bowl on a trivet in a pan of boiling water. There should be just enough water to come halfway up the bowl.

☛ Steam the pudding for 4 hours, topping up the water periodically.

Summer Pudding

INGREDIENTS

SERVES 6—8

6–8 slices white bread

3–4 cups/675 g/1½ lb soft fruit

½ cup/100 g/4 oz sugar

2 tbsp/30 ml water

PREPARATION

☛ Remove the crusts from the bread and cut into fingers. Cover the base and sides of a 1 litre/2 pint soufflé dish or pudding bowl, saving enough pieces of bread to make a lid for the pudding.

☛ Place the fruit in a heavy-bottomed pan. Sprinkle with sugar and water. Cook over a very low heat until the sugar has dissolved and the fruit is soft but not mushy. The juices should be running freely.

☛ Strain the fruit, reserving the juice. Pour two spoonfuls of juice over the bread in the base of the bowl. Spoon the fruit into the bread case. Pour over all but 6 spoonfuls of the juice.

☛ Arrange the remaining bread fingers over the top of the fruit. Pour over the remaining juice.

☛ Place a dish, small enough to fit inside the rim of the bowl, on top of the pudding. Press down with heavy cans or weights. Put the summer pudding into the refrigerator and leave for at least 8 hours.

☛ Just before you are ready to eat the pudding, remove the weights and the dish. Place a serving dish over the pudding and turn upside down to unmould.

TO SERVE

Serve with whipped cream or pouring (light or heavy) cream.